JL KING

FULL CIRCLE

Loving. Living. Life.
After The Down Low

BROWN GIRLS PUBLISHING

Houston, Texas * Washington, D.C.

Full Circle © 2014 by JL King
Brown Girls Publishing, LLC
www.browngirlspublishing.com

ISBN: 9781625174307

First Brown Girls Publishing LLC trade printing

Manufactured and Printed in the United States of America

INTRODUCTION

When my publishers and I started talking about the title of this book, my final book, my last performance, my 'this is it' book, I didn't want to have the words 'down low' on the cover. I was so over that tagline that has followed me and haunted me for the past ten years.

But even though the title of this book didn't readily come, I knew that it would. I was confident about that because I knew all I had to do was pray.

Praying is like breathing for me. I pray on everything that I do. So, I told the publishers not to worry, I was going to pray, and I would get back to them with something.

There was one thing I knew for sure about this book and this title. . . everything had to be bigger and better than *On The Down Low*, my first book that is still bigger than me. And still selling like hotcakes, still a top seller internationally, still talked about everywhere, including college campuses where it is required reading in 49 universities. *On the Down Low* is still the book that has been credited with changing the definition of sexuality and what is 'gay.' And not only that, but *On the Down Low* is still the book that can cause major controversy just by bringing up the title in discussion. Talking about this book will always lead to all kinds of debates and battles. It is still the book that has sparked and still sparks movies and movements.

On the Down Low is still the book that made JL a household name, still the book that has been both a burden and a blessing to me and my family, still the book that has been a source of joy, but also a lot of pain for me, too.

So this, my very last book, had to be able to back all of that up. It would be the tenth anniversary of my coming out and the title, the cover, everything had to be right—including who I chose to publish the book.

There were many publishers I could have gone to, but I wanted this to be published by my friends, Victoria Christopher Murray and ReShonda Tate Billingsley. I respect them as businesswomen and authors. Victoria and I have a long history of supporting each other and I love her caring spirit. Often, I tell aspiring authors to watch her—she is where they should aspire to reach. When she and ReShonda started Brown Girls Publishing/Brown Girls Books, I knew that the two of them would partner with me to make this book an even bigger success than the last.

So, I started tossing titles around in my head. And then, the name FULL CIRCLE hit me. FULL CIRCLE was perfect because that is exactly what had happened in my life. I'd come full circle. And though my journey on earth is not complete, this part of my life is. Thinking about this book in terms of having made a full circle, having come all the way around, would challenge me to share everything, every part of my life. I wanted to write a "tell all" that would *tell all* of my story. I wanted the world to hear my side—from Oprah's couch, to instant celebrity status. I wanted to tell the story of the full circle journey from being a straight man to being a gay man. And I wanted to share all the details, not to be gratuitous, but to give everyone insight into what happens when a man begins to live in his truth and has to learn the lessons as his life is unfolding.

Though many think that they know me because of one book and two appearances on Oprah, no one knows all of me. I have remained quiet on so many things when all I really wanted to do was shout out the truth. I've wanted to clear up the lies that have been written and spoken about me. But until now, I've remained silent.

But no more. I am ready to speak. I am ready to tell the truths that I never shared before. Like the truth about the sexual partners that I met at church. These guys became my boys and we ended up having sex with each other. It didn't matter that most of us were either married or had girlfriends.

I wanted to tell the truth of the married minister that I had a relationship with. The minister who died of AIDS after having unprotected sex with me and everyone else.

I wanted to tell the truth of the sex parties, the men I met (famous and infamous) and how none of us considered ourselves gay.

Clearly, I didn't create the term down low; I was just chosen to be the face of this lifestyle, the man chosen to write this story. Thus, the name of this book. Because once I came to that realization, I'd come all the way around from being a man who was hiding to now knowing that I had to tell everything—including that I am a gay man.

So that's why I've written this book, this legacy. It is the truth that I am finally willing to face completely. And this is proof that I truly have come FULL CIRCLE.

PROLOGUE

May 2004

When I left Harpo Studios that beautiful sunny morning in the limo that Oprah used for her guests, I was in a daze. In the limo with me was my daughter, Ebony, and two of the sisters who were scheduled to be on the show. I was quiet and still in shock that I had just revealed to the world that I had been living a double life and had cheated on my wife with other men. And even with that, I didn't consider myself gay. Now, everybody who thought they knew me, had heard the truth. My family, friends, church family, and co-workers were probably all stunned. Even my trusted close best friends who I grew up with and were sure that they knew Jimmy King had heard things today that they'd never known.

I had told Oprah that I was a monster, representing all those other monsters out there—men who destroyed and infected women with HIV. I had even told the talk show queen that I could pick any man in the audience and have sex with him if I really want to.

Damn! What had I been thinking? I couldn't believe I'd said that. Where did that all come from anyway? Who'd taken over my mind and body?

The shy Jimmy King from Springfield, Ohio was not the same man who had just revealed all of his deepest secrets to the world. I couldn't even process all that had happened and as the limo drove us back to the hotel, I didn't want to talk about it. All I wanted to do was throw up and jump in front of a bus. I had a feeling that my appearance on Oprah was going to change my life. Little did I know how much. My life and all that I knew would never be the same after the one hour I spent on Oprah's couch.

CHAPTER 1

Where do I begin?

*M*any believe that my story began in 2004 when I was introduced to the world on *The Oprah Winfrey Show*. But my journey began way before then. Really, you could say that it began when I was nine years old and I had my very first sexual experience with my cousin. Or when I was in junior high school and my mother found a note in my book bag that I'd written to a fellow male student telling him that I loved him. Or maybe it began on the day my wife found me in bed with another man.

You could say that my journey began at any of those moments. But I say, that my journey toward the realization and acceptance of who I was began in 2001. It was in 2001 when I was fired from my job at the Columbus, Ohio Urban League. I'd been a Director, heading up the program to help ex offenders fill out applications, write resumes, and interview for jobs as they assimilated back into society. It was a great position that allowed me to really make a difference in people's lives, but I was working there when my life truly changed.

I'd been hired into that position back in 1998 by the president of the Urban League. When he hired me, that job had come right on time. I had been at such a low point in my life. I was unemployed, broke, living out of my car, and I didn't see any kind of brightness in my future. My life was so bad that suicidal thoughts plagued me day and night. I was at my end, so why not end it all? God didn't love me; that was clear by the way my life was going. And even though I'd been raised in the church and had loved God all of my life, I began to question whether God was even real. How could He be when I was suffering so much? I was done with faith and with God.

I felt like I was in the desert and in fact, that's what I began to call this period of my life—my 40 days and 40 nights. I was alone, hungry, thirsting, completely without any friends and there was no family that I could go to. I was totally fucked up. That is the only way I can describe me and that time. Lost.

But, even though my faith wavered, even though I thought about taking my life, God showed up when I was ready to give up. And He came to me in the form of a job.

I had stopped at the cleaners one day to pick up a suit that I had dropped off so that I could at least have something to wear as I looked for a job. After I gave the lady my ticket, I glanced over my shoulder. I was checking out my car, praying that the repo man wouldn't get it while I was in here. I had a

1998 Buick Park Avenue, and that was more than just a car. That was my shelter.

But I couldn't focus on the car because just as I turned around, the door opened and in walked a man—Sam Gresham.

We had been friends just a few years before when I was working in corporate America, sitting on corporate boards, including the Urban League, and working with the city of Columbus to raise money for different programs. I was considered a rising star. Everyone knew my name, wanted my number and called on me when they needed to make something happen.

Sam Gresham was one of the people in Columbus who thought of me as a mover and shaker. We were social equals... back then. But so much had happened in my life and one quick glance at his tailored suit and his spit-shined shoes let me know that we weren't equals any more.

Quickly, I turned my head and lowered it at the same time, trying to hide my face. I was so embarrassed and didn't want him to see me. What would I say? What would he say? I wanted to run right out of there, but I needed my suit. So I made myself as small as I could and kept my head down. If I was lucky, he wouldn't see the little man trying to hide in the corner.

But then, I heard, "Jim? Jim King?"

I was busted. Even though I tried to pretend that I didn't hear him, I couldn't ignore him. So, I turned around.

"Hey, Sam," I said with as much strength and enthusiasm as I could.

"It is you," he said, like he was glad to see me.

I figured that he was. I would've been glad to see him, too, if I wasn't in my desert.

"Jim, where have you been? I haven't seen you in a couple of years."

He was right about that. I had disappeared. He didn't know where I'd been and he didn't know my story.

"So, what are you doing in town?" he asked, still doing all of the talking.

"I'm just here. . ." That was all I said and it seemed like it was enough for him.

"Well, what are you doing now? Where are you working?"

Of course, I wasn't going to tell him that I was homeless, hoping that somehow my life was going to turn around. "I just got through with a contract where I was teaching at state prisons," I said, telling him about my last position. I left out the part about how I'd been fired for making sexual advances to my clients. That was the reason I was homeless now.

I'd had a fat contract with the state to provide GED classes and pre-release employment training to inmates. So I was inside the prison constantly and in the middle of thousands of men.

That was not a good place for me to be. Not with the sexual appetite I had for men. And those inmates could read me. They knew who I was by the way my eyes lingered on them just a little too long, or the way I fidgeted when one of them sat in my office, shirtless. They could tell that I was turned on and that I was fighting my own desires toward men.

So, the inmates fed on that. That's what prisoners do. They seek out staff members who can be exploited. They find their weaknesses and go after that because once a prisoner knows your weakness, they can use it to their advantage. My weakness was front and center—I was a man who loved men. It wasn't difficult for the inmates to see and the inmates came after me. I was set up, but it was my fault.

Sam interrupted my reflection back in time when he asked, "Really? So you're finished with that contract?"

I nodded.

"This is great," he said. "I just received a two-year grant with the Urban League to work with inmates. You and I need to talk," he said. He reached into his pocket, and then gave me his business card. "When can you get by to see me?"

I wanted to tell him that we could talk now, but I didn't want to appear as desperate as I was. So, I told him that I'd go down to the Urban League the next day. Then, I walked out of the cleaners, not stopping at my car. I didn't want him to see me get into the car that had everything that I owned piled high in the back. So, I went around the corner and waited for him to leave before I got into my car.

The next day, Sam interviewed and then hired me to work with prisoners upon their release. The job was for very little money, but it was a job! I still had to live in my car because even with this job I couldn't afford an apartment, not to mention, I wasn't sure I'd even be able to get an apartment since my credit was shot. But at least with this job, I was on my way to having some stability back in my life. I was so grateful to be given another chance. This was my second or maybe even my third chance at getting it right, and I really wanted to do it this time.

The job was wonderful for the three years that I held the position. I ended up getting fired for the same reason that I'd been fired from my last one—because I made a sexual advance to one of my clients/students.

It was a vicious, ugly pattern with me. I was still trying to hide my sexuality and it always got the best of me, especially when I was around a lot of good looking black men.

I should have learned my lesson. After being fired twice, you would think that I would stay away from certain employment positions or just stop trying to hide who I was. But I didn't learn. I continued to hide, I continued to make advances, and I continued to get fired. Opportunity after opportunity, after opportunity. Lessons I should have learned, but I didn't; because I was hardheaded.

That was a trait that had followed me all my life. From the time I was a child, my hard headedness haunted me. And it cost me. But not before it hurt so many people. And for that, I will always be sorry.

But to understand me, to understand how I arrived at this place where I'd hurt so many people, you'll have to know who I was and where it all began.

CHAPTER 2

The Beginning of it All

I was born on December 4 in Springfield, Ohio to Louis and Lillie King. My parents had migrated from the south; Mom grew up in Cartersville, Georgia, about two hours north of Atlanta and my dad was from a small country town in Alabama called Browns, right outside of Salem, Alabama.

My dad, like so many other black men, journeyed to the North because of the better employment opportunities. So a few years after my parents were married, they ended up in Springfield, Ohio, where my father began what would be a long career working for the government.

My mother worked as a domestic for white families because she wanted to, not because she had to. What my mother wanted most was to have children. By that time, her only sister had three and my mother and father had none. It wasn't because they hadn't tried, though. Before I was born, my mother gave birth to five stillborn babies. So when I came along, their first living child, I was a true miracle and the greatest gift for Louis and Lillie.

As you can imagine, my mother was very protective of me. She wouldn't even allow anyone to hold me for the first few months of my life. No one could get too close to her baby, James Louis King. I was named after my father's dad, James, and my middle name was my father's. Three years after me, my brother, Ronald L. King was born.

My parents worked hard to provide a wonderful life for me and my brother. While my father continued working for the government, my mother left the domestic work behind and worked as an elevator operator at the Sears in downtown Springfield.

They were hardworking, God-fearing people who were greatly respected in our community. They raised us in the church, where my father was a deacon and my mother was in the choir. Outside of church, they did their best to give their sons all kinds of opportunities. I took piano lessons, was in the Boy Scouts, and participated in every other after-school program my parents could think of. There was hardly anything that I wanted that I didn't receive. I've been called spoiled, and that was very true. I was a spoiled Mama's boy until the day that my mother died.

Even though my parents were outgoing, I wasn't. I was quite shy, a chubby kid who didn't have many friends because I preferred to hang out with my mother more than anyone else.

I loved being in the kitchen helping her cook. And when she went shopping, I was all over it. That was my favorite thing to do with my mother. I loved to dress, so my mom and I would spend hours in the stores.

That was how I became so close to my mother, but I could never find that kind of closeness with my father. I knew that he loved me, and I knew that I could have gone to him if I needed anything physically, but emotionally, it didn't feel like my dad was there for me. Like I said, he loved me, but he was old school. His job was to take care of the family. That was it—he was the provider. It was my mother's job to give the children anything else they needed.

So, while my dad was my dad, my mom was my girl! I could go to her, I could talk to her about anything.

The one thing I didn't talk about to anybody was school. I wasn't a good student, really, I was quite bad. (And I hated English so it's ironic that I became a writer!) I wasn't a jock, I didn't play sports at all; that was my brother's turf and that was where my brother and my dad bonded. I wasn't popular because you had to have friends to be popular, and like I said, I didn't have many. I had tons of cousins, though, ten to be exact, and so I hung out with them.

My cousins and my brother and I were like siblings. I was especially close to my male cousins. There were five of them and TJ and I were about the same age. I was closest to him, closer than I was even to my own brother; TJ and I did everything together.

One night when TJ was spending the night with us, I laid in my bed thinking about him. We had been outside playing all day, doing nothing really, just hanging out. But we'd really had a good time.

As I laid there, I thought about how I really loved TJ. Of course, I loved everyone else, but the love I had for TJ felt different. Very different.

Then, my thoughts of my cousin wandered. To this day, I can't tell you where the thought came from or why it manifested at that moment. It was as if the thought just dropped into my head and once it was there, I couldn't let it go.

I couldn't stop thinking about my cousin's penis and I wanted to see it. The longer I laid there, the longer that thought stayed with me. I had to see it!

We had never played any games like that before, had never exposed ourselves to each other. Truly, I'm telling you, I don't know where that urge came from. But it was so strong that I got up and tiptoed across the room to where he was sleeping in my brother's bed. I stood there for a moment, and watched him. TJ was fast asleep.

My heart pounded as I leaned over and slowly, as easily as I could, I slipped down his underwear until I could see his penis. For a moment, I stood there, just staring at it in the dark. And then...I bent over and put his penis in my mouth. I didn't do it for very long; not only was I afraid that TJ might wake up, but I was really scared of my mother. My parents' room was across the hall and both bedroom doors were open. I knew I would be in big trouble if she caught me.

So after a couple of seconds, I jumped right back into my bed, excited on so many levels. I got to see my cousin's penis! I got to taste it! And, I got away with it!

That was probably what turned me on the most. The risk. The idea that I could have been caught, but I wasn't.

I probably laid in that bed for more than an hour before I fell asleep. The next morning, I was a little afraid of what my cousin would say, but TJ never said a word. It was as if he didn't know what had happened. I wasn't sure if he knew or not, but I never said a word.

I guess that was the beginning of my desire for men, and my keeping secrets. It started when I was just nine years old.

After that, I can say that I was always attracted to the male physique. It was more curiosity than anything else because for many years, I never did anything beyond those few seconds with my cousin.

Though in junior high school, I did have sort of a male encounter. Another student in my class, a white boy, started sending me notes. We exchanged notes back and forth; he told me how much he liked me, I told him that I loved him. That was as far as it went. Just notes that we sent each other and nothing else. But one day, I left one of those notes in my pants pocket. And while doing the laundry, my mother found it in my pocket and brought the note to me.

"This was in your jeans," my mother said. Then, she gave me one of those black mama looks, but she didn't say another word.

That was it—the full extent of my experiences with boys and by the time I got to high school, I was over it (or so I thought) and I turned to girls.

I still didn't have a lot of friends, but I did have my little crew...my cousin and four other boys who lived in the same 'hood. We didn't do much, just hung out, listened to music, and talked to girls—you know, all the things that teenage boys do.

My parents were really cool with that. They didn't push education on my brother and me. As long as we attended church, came home at our curfew, had an after school job, stayed out of trouble, and didn't make babies (that was my father's big thing,) they were happy.

I made it through those four years of high school, just barely. I thanked God for getting my high school diploma because I just didn't like school. I was a poor student and the fact that I had made it through was good enough. There was no thought of college in my mind. My studying days were over.

But as a high school graduate, I had to do something and I didn't have many options; just the military, really. Several of my older cousins had entered the military and that seemed pretty exciting to me. Not only would going into the military allow me to leave Springfield, but I would get to see the world at the same time. I was ready to go.

I was leaving Springfield with lots of lessons from school, from church, from my parents; I was well-equipped. But the thing is, when lessons are there, you have to take heed to them and I wasn't one of those children who learned that. As a child, no one could tell me anything; how could they? I knew everything!

Looking back, I can only shake my head at the number of mistakes I made because of that hard-headed character flaw. Since I never wanted to listen, I never learned. I walked around like a know-it-all. I was young, I was smart enough, and I could take care of myself.

But being mature has nothing to do with taking care of yourself physically. That, I could do well. It was in the other areas, especially emotionally, where I was lacking.

There are so many things that I wish that I could take back. So many times when I wish I'd listened, when I wish I'd learned. Being hard-headed only made my life more difficult.

So, I left Springfield, Ohio young, dumb, and destined for failure. I didn't know it then, but I was headed for some really hard falls and unfortunately, I was going to bring quite a few other folks down with me.

CHAPTER 3

Growing Up Fast!

I was going into the United States Air Force!

I had enrolled and was set to go to basic training six months after I graduated from high school. Talk about not being able to wait; I was anxious to be out on my own.

And the major reason I wanted to be on my own—Brenda Stone!

Brenda Stone was my high school girlfriend and I wanted to marry her. I met her when she was a sophomore. I was a junior and it was love at first sight for me. Even though I still found myself sometimes attracted to guys, that had nothing to do with the feelings that I had for girls, specifically Brenda. With guys, it was a sexual attraction. With Brenda, it was in my heart. I was in love!

We'd dated all through high school, and really from our first date, I knew that she was going to be my wife. That's the life I wanted—a wife with lots of babies and Brenda was the one.

From the moment I met her, Brenda was amazing. She was a fox with big legs, a short cropped Afro, beautiful lips. Not only did she come from a good family from our neighborhood, but she was smart, smart, smart. Brenda was my future.

She was still in high school, completing her senior year when I enrolled in the Air Force, but I had a plan—I would go to basic training, get my first assignment, then come back, marry Brenda, and take her with me.

So while Brenda and I made plans to get married, I headed off to Lackland Air Force base in Texas.

Being in the USAF was my first time being away from my parents. It was my first taste of real freedom. I was away from all the rules and regulations—at least the rules and regulations of my parents. Of course, the military had their own rules, but I still felt free. In this new world, I was treated like an adult. There weren't always people watching—at least when I wasn't on the clock. And part of that freedom meant that I could explore my sexual curiosity.

I wasn't the only one who was away from home for the first time. Everyone there was just like me—young men who were right out of high school. There were thousands of them, and those old desires that I'd had as a young boy began to bubble up inside. Those thoughts I'd had about my cousin when I was nine, consumed me once again. It was hard to suppress my feelings when I was around all those men.

The first time I took a group shower and I was in that space with about twenty-five other airmen, I just about lost my mind. The shower space was not that large, so we were piled in there together, and I was able to freely stare at all of those bodies. I had never seen so many naked men at one time.

That first day in the shower, I allowed my eyes to roam through the group and study all the men. I found five black guys who were all well endowed and I decided right then, they were going to be my friends.

It didn't concern me that I had a girlfriend at home. In my mind, my desire for men had nothing to do with her. I loved Brenda and I knew what I felt for guys wasn't the same.

Not that I was ever going to act upon those feelings. It wasn't like you could just hook up with guys. Not in the Air Force or any of the military divisions. Uncle Sam was not having that. There was a zero tolerance for homosexuality in the military.

So because I wanted to remain in the Air Force, I had to hide (not repress) my sexuality. There was no way to repress the strong desires that seemed to be getting stronger daily. My sexuality was going to come out. Period. I knew that; I just didn't know when.

CHAPTER 4

Love Against the Odds

I completed my basic training and returned home. And the first thing I wanted to do was marry Brenda.

"But we can't get married," she said. "I'm still in high school."

"That doesn't matter," I told her. "We can still do it." I wanted to do it right away since I was only going to be home for a few months before I had to leave for my first military assignment. And if we were married, then Brenda could go with me.

But when we talked to her parents, those plans quickly changed. Brenda's parents were not happy. Not that I expected them to be, but they were more adamant than I anticipated.

"You can't get married," her father told me and Brenda. "You're still in high school."

"But she'll be graduating in a few months," I protested.

No matter what I said, though, Brenda's parents weren't hearing it. It was clear that the dreams they had for their daughter didn't include a wedding ring from me. It was only because Brenda sat there by my side and insisted that she did want to get married, that her parents finally gave in. But there was a caveat.

"First of all, this is not happening until you graduate from high school," her father said.

I expected him to say that and I could live with it. She was only a few months away from graduating anyway.

"And secondly, you still have to go straight to college."

Now that part, I wasn't expecting. I wasn't sure what that would mean. I wanted Brenda to go with me to wherever I was going to be assigned, but if her parents wanted her in college, then that would mean she would probably stay in Springfield.

Those were her parents' rules, though, and if we wanted to be married, we had to abide by them. At least we would be married.

But if Brenda's parents were tough, my parents, or I should say, my mother was impossible. My mother was totally against my marriage.

"No, Jimmy. You don't need to be getting married."

I didn't have to ask her; I knew all of her reasons for saying that. First of all, I was still her baby, her miracle baby. And just because I was grown, it didn't change the fact that my mother still saw me that way. She was still so protective.

"You're too young," she said, giving me a reason. "And Brenda...."

My mother didn't finish her sentence, she just shook her head. She didn't like Brenda, though it really wasn't personal. She didn't like her because Brenda was taking her baby away.

"It's a mistake, Jimmy." My mother looked me in the eye and said, "You shouldn't get married. The marriage won't last and people will get hurt."

And there was her best reason. It was unspoken, but my mother knew I shouldn't become anybody's husband. Not with what she knew about me. My mother knew what I wouldn't admit and what she wouldn't say out loud. I was gay.

But, this was one of those times when I was hardheaded. I knew what I wanted—and that was to marry Brenda. No one was going to get hurt. I loved Brenda too much to hurt her. So I was going to do what I wanted to do. Despite Brenda's parents and my mother's objections, we got married.

The year was 1973 and we had a small ceremony in the living room of Brenda's parents home. Although our parents were there, the morning of our wedding, I wasn't so sure that my mother was going to show up. She meant what she said about me and Brenda and our marriage and she was not happy.

As I was getting ready that morning, my mother cried and cried and cried. My father told me that she didn't even want to get out of bed. She acted as if someone died! When I went to talk to her, all she would tell me was that I shouldn't get married.

It took my father to convince her. I'm sure my father thought that I was kinda young, too, but he supported me and Brenda.

He told my mother, "You've got to let him go. Jimmy's a man, now. He has to make his own decisions."

Finally, my mother agreed to attend my wedding, though she made a protest move—she wore pants. That was a big deal because she never wore pants. But she showed up in this loud red pinstriped pants suit. And she didn't stay long. The minister had barely said, "You may now kiss the bride," before my mom was out the door.

At least she came, even though she never changed her mind, even though she continued to tell me that I was making the biggest mistake of my life.

I kept telling my mother that she was the one who was wrong. I knew what I was doing. No matter what she said, she was wrong and I was right.

Of course, if I had just listened to my mother, if I had just thought about it for a little while, I would have known that my mother was so, so right. Mothers always know. Mothers always know their children and Mrs. Lillie Mae King knew her son was queer, which was the word that was used in the seventies. Whatever the word—queer, punk, gay—my mother knew that I was different. And in her way, she did everything she could to stop me.

But she couldn't. I got married. I said my vows to love and to cherish Brenda Stone. I promised to honor my new wife until death parted us. That was my plan, but you already know my marriage didn't last. Like my mother said, people were hurt. Like my mother knew, it was all because of my sexuality. So much pain could have been avoided if I had just listened. So much would have been different if I wasn't so hardheaded.

But I didn't listen. And I didn't learn to listen for many years to come.

CHAPTER 5

Just a Grown Up Kid

I was assigned to an Air Force base in Upper Penn, Michigan. Kincheloe Air Force Base. It was a small Strategic Air Command base and the only black folk living there were military families.

There was not a lot to remember nor a lot to like about Kincheloe. It was in the middle of nowhere, on the upper peninsula of the state. Being so far North meant that the winters were harsh. The frigid temperatures were brutal and the snow was massive. It wasn't where I wanted to go, but that was where I was assigned for the next two years.

Like we had promised her parents, Brenda stayed behind in Springfield and enrolled at Wright State, though she only stayed there for a semester before she transferred to Central State University. I was so proud of my wife. I didn't like that she wasn't with me, but she stayed on campus, and we talked on the phone every day. Every few days, we wrote letters to each other.

Being in love and being married didn't stop those internal desires that I had for men, though. I still hadn't acted out on those desires, but I certainly wanted to. I looked at naked men every chance I got. And living in that dorm in Kincheloe gave me chances every day.

My roommate was a guy named, Travis, from Detroit. Travis was married, too, and our room became the place for everyone to hang out after work. Guys were making it really difficult for me, coming by our room half-naked, hanging out in nothing but their underwear.

I did the best I could to make sure they never saw my eyes lingering on them for too long. I certainly didn't want any of the guys to peep what I was feeling. So I struggled to keep my secret.

Staying silent and hiding was the most difficult thing I've ever done. It took everything inside of me not to approach one of the guys for oral sex. I wasn't going to do it, though. Not only did I not want to be rejected, but I didn't want to get discharged for being a faggot. So, I just looked, but never touched.

Part of keeping my secret was to create a persona that was so far away from what I was feeling. So that no one would suspect what was in my heart, I dated the hottest, sexiest female airmen on the base. And it worked. My reputation was that I was a ladies' man and that I was hitting all of them every chance I had.

Of course, that was just talk; it was all about my rep. Yes, I dated, but I didn't have sex with any of those women. I didn't desire to, and I was married. If I had done anything with any woman, that would've been cheating on Brenda and I loved my wife too much to do that.

But as far as men were concerned, that was different. And those men living around me made it really tough. Especially when my friends and I teased each other. There was one incident when I got into a debate with this dude and after we went through a couple of verbal rounds, he said, "Man, Jimmy, suck my dick!"

He was kidding, of course. But he even went so far as to pull his penis out of his pants. Now, he was a short brother, but he was well endowed and as I stood there and stared at him, he had no idea how bad I wanted to take him up on that offer.

And he wasn't the only one that I was crushing on. There was this guy from Memphis who was married with three kids. Since I was away from Brenda, he and his wife adopted me. They were a real nice couple that looked out for me, inviting me to their base trailer all the time for dinner. Whenever I was over there, his wife would talk to Brenda on the phone, while the guy and I just hung out. But while they were looking out for me because I'd left my wife back in Ohio, I was doing everything that I could to be around this dude.

He was so cute, and I was so smitten that I would do whatever I had to do to get them to invite me to their place.

The dude was straight and he had no idea that I wanted to have sex with him. I never let on that I did. In fact, the entire two years that I was away, I didn't let on to anyone.

But just because I controlled my desires, didn't mean they weren't there. And it didn't mean that they were going away. All I'd done was hide who I really was. It was going to have to come out sooner or later.

And it did. At my very next assignment.

CHAPTER 6

And so it begins...

When my assignment in Michigan ended, Uncle Sam sent me to a NATO unit in Izmir, Turkey. Izmir is a large metropolis, the third most populous city in Turkey. Izmir didn't have a typical Air Force base. Instead of military personnel living on the base, we all lived among the citizens in this Muslim city.

I was going to be in Izmir for two years and this time, I was going to have my wife with me. Brenda had finished two years of college and though I knew her parents wanted her to stay at home and get her degree, she was twenty-one now. We wanted to be together.

I went to Turkey first to find and secure an apartment for us. This was going to be our first time living together and I wanted our place to be special; at least, as special as it could be so far away from home.

It only took me a few days to find a really nice two-bedroom apartment on the tenth floor of a new high rise. I called Brenda, told her about it, and she had to trust me that she would like it, since this was decades before the Internet. But we were both excited that she would be joining me within a few months.

Not living on a military base helped me a lot. I wasn't around a lot of men. Of course, I was when I was at work, but living in an apartment alone was far better than being in a dorm where I was around naked and half-dressed men all the time.

And now that Brenda was going to be with me, I wanted to get my feelings for men under control. Truly, I wanted my desire to only be for my wife and I had prayed and prayed and prayed that God would take away those desires so that my focus would be on Brenda.

At first, I thought it was working. I thought that my living arrangements were keeping me safe. After all, though I was living among the natives, I didn't speak the language. So there was no way for me to get into any kind of trouble.

At least that's what I thought until the evening when I got on the bus to go home and sat across from this really handsome Turkish guy. He was young, about my age, with dark, sexy features. I remember his eyes the most. With his eyes, he spoke to me and as we sat on that bus, we stared and spoke silently to each other.

Not a verbal word was exchanged between us, but when I stood up to get off, he followed me. He followed me straight to my apartment and for the first time ever, I was with a man... in Turkey.

Now by definition, we didn't have sex. All we did was bump and grind with our clothes on, like we were sex-starved teenagers. And, he performed oral sex on me.

But it felt like sex to me. It was the first time I felt a man's hard body against mine; something I'd been lusting for so long.

It was really crazy—the way we met, the fact that we couldn't even communicate. But what was the craziest thing was that being with him was such a high risk. First of all, I had no idea who this guy was. I had a complete stranger in my apartment. And, I was in the military, living in a Muslim country where practicing homosexuality could lead to death. That alone should have been enough to stop me. But it didn't.

I met up with that guy day after day to lay with him and fondle him, and have him fondle and perform oral sex on me. The need for those feelings, the need to be touched by a man overrode my good and common sense.

I continued that affair until Brenda arrived and then, I stopped...cold turkey. I turned my focus and attention to my wife. She was happy to be with me and loved the apartment. And like me, she was anxious to begin our new life as a young married couple.

Once again I hoped and prayed that every desire I had for a man would be taken away. I wanted to only love my wife.

Living in Turkey was not easy for us. The country was at war with Greece. And there was always some kind of alert issued to Americans: Stay in the house...Be careful going out. Oftentimes, the Turkish government would turn off our electricity or we would have no water.

But even with the hardships of being so far away from home and living in a country at war, Turkey was a beautiful place. Since Turkey is in both Europe and Asia, it is rich with the cultures of both continents. From the lushness of the countryside to the architectural history that is so prevalent in Turkey, Brenda and I had a wonderful time exploring the country.

We built a life, meeting and socializing with other American couples who lived in our building or those we met at the military store. The Army and Air Force personnel were stationed together.

We were only in Turkey for only a few months when we found out that Brenda was pregnant. There are no words to describe how ecstatic I was. I was going to be a father! Brenda was happy about it, too, but honestly, being so young and pregnant was hard on her. Not the pregnancy, per se, but being so far away from home and everyone who loved her.

But the military doctor checked her out, gave her a clean bill of health, and Brenda went about the task of becoming a wonderful wife and preparing for our child. I loved the way she'd turned our apartment into a home, from the way she furnished it, to the way she cooked meals that made me think of being back in Ohio, Brenda was on it.

We started working on the second bedroom, turning it into a nursery and Brenda took up knitting. She began working on a blanket for our baby and reading everything that she could so that she would be ready.

I wanted to be as supportive as I could to my wife and I tried to be a good husband. Every day, I did my eight hours of duty, then rushed home to be with her. Brenda and I didn't do much; either we'd hang out together or with other couples. And then, there was our faith. We'd become even stronger in our faith while we were in Turkey, and I was glad about that. Brenda and I went to church and Bible Study weekly.

Maybe that was why I felt little temptation to be with other men at that time. Maybe it was church, and my wife; I don't know. Whatever it was, I didn't have those urges and for the first year, it was enough for me to be with just Brenda and to concentrate on the impending arrival of our first child.

⁂

As I mentioned, we weren't living on a military base in Turkey, so for the birth, Brenda was flown to the closest military base. About a week before Brenda's delivery date, the USAF flew us to Ankara Air Force Base. Brenda was admitted into the hospital and I was put up at the on-base hotel to wait on the birth. There were lots of other young airmen there, also waiting on their babies. But while I was always friendly, my focus was on my wife. Each day, I spent as much time as they allowed with Brenda at the hospital.

The night her water broke, I received a call from the hospital and was told that it was time. I dashed over to the hospital, but Brenda was already in the delivery room when I arrived. I wanted to rush right in there to be with her, but I wasn't allowed.

I paced and paced in the waiting room, with all kinds of thoughts going through my head. I was about to be a father. What kind of father would I be? Were we going to have a boy or a girl? What did the future hold for my child? For Brenda? For me?

It was only a few hours later when the doctor came out and told me that I was the father of a little girl that I was able to breathe. If I didn't want to see Brenda so bad, I would've just dropped to my knees right then and thanked God. But I ran into the room and there was my wife—and my beautiful baby girl. Talk about love at first sight. Everything about our baby was perfect: from her thick head of hair to her brown eyes that tried to focus on me. This was the greatest gift that I'd ever received in my life.

Looking into my daughter's beautiful brown eyes, made my own fill with tears. I was so in love with Brenda, I was so in love with our new daughter. I knew that there would be few moments in my life that would ever be better than this.

We stayed in Ankara for a few days and then, we were flown back to Izmir to begin our new life as a family: Brenda, and I...and Ebony Markis King!

CHAPTER 7

Torn Between Two Lovers

I was a new husband and now, I was a new father. The only thing that could have made this time better was to be home in Ohio with family so that I could be around other people who loved me and we could celebrate this together.

And then...just as I was settling into my newest role as a father, temptation strolled right back into my life. I was sucked back in, seduced by a young, beautiful brother from Texas.

Carlos was stationed in Izmir, but even though he was married, he'd come to Turkey alone. His wife had stayed behind in Texas to take care of their son.

Carlos was just gorgeous to me. With his light-skin, light-brown colored eyes, and eyelashes that went on for days, I had a hard time holding back all the feelings that rushed straight to my penis every time I saw him.

Because he was alone, Carlos spent a lot of time at our place and he quickly became like a brother to both Brenda and me. Besides just hanging out and having dinner with us, Carlos was also part of our Bible studies and readings.

I really did try to fight it, but I had a big thing for this brother. We never talked about it, but we had these signals, these gestures that we would share. We would play footies under the table when we were having dinner. Or we would accidentally rub up against each other when we passed by.

Then, it progressed.

It started when he would sometimes spend the night with us when it was pretty late and he didn't want to go back to his apartment. Of course, he used being late as an excuse to stay. That was fine with me because I never wanted him to leave.

On the nights when Carlos stayed, I would kiss Brenda good night, tell her that I loved her. Then go into Ebony's room, kiss her good night, tell her that I loved her. And finally, I'd go into the living room where Carlos would be sitting on the couch in his underwear just waiting for me. We didn't have an American TV channel, so watching TV was out. That meant we spent much of our time listening to Radio Free America stations, or just sitting on the sofa, talking.

That's how it began, but pretty quickly, it escalated. Not to full blown sex, but I would sit and fondle him before we ended the night with a kiss. And I would tell Carlos that I loved him.

I really did love him. Even though Brenda was in our bedroom asleep, I was kissing this man, stroking his penis, and telling him that I loved him just like I loved my wife. It may be hard for others to understand, and I get that. But, I'm telling the truth when I say I loved both of them.

Our relationship continued this way for two years until Carlos transferred back to the States. He was going home to San Antonio, Texas.

From the moment I found out that he was leaving me, I was depressed. And, I'm telling you that when he actually left, I was so hurt, I cried. My wife thought that my pain came from being in a foreign country, so far away from home, and losing my best friend, the only real friend I had in Turkey.

But what she didn't know was that my hurt came from a deeper place. It was so much more. For the first time in my life, I was in love with a man and Brenda had no idea. She didn't know that my heart was hurting. The problem was I needed my man in my life and when he left, I could hardly function. I wasn't able to sleep, didn't want to eat. The only thing was that it did bring Brenda and I a little closer. I found solace in her arms, though it was not enough.

Soon after, though, I found a solution. I requested that my next assignment be in San Antonio, TX where he lived.

The USAF assigned me to Randolf Air Force Base outside of San Antonio. I was so excited. Not only was I going home, but I was going to be with my man, too.

CHAPTER 8

A Wonderful Life

*A*fter two years in Turkey, Brenda and I were back home. We weren't in Ohio where I knew Brenda wanted us to be. But Texas was good enough for her, and it's what I needed.

Carlos didn't extend his service time; he got out of the Air Force. But even though I had considered getting out of the military, I reenlisted for four more years just so that I could be close to him. Or else, I wouldn't have had any reason to be in San Antonio.

So we were back together again. He, as a civilian with his wife and son. And, I was military with a wife and daughter. It was perfect. Carlos was even Ebony's godfather.

Our relationship grew under the nose of our wives. Not that either one of them was naive or stupid. Carlos and I took great care to be deceptive. Since our wives became such good friends, we'd send them out together on shopping sprees and adventures with the kids. Sometimes, we'd keep the kids home so that the two of them could have girlfriend time together. We did a great job of covering up. We were the perfect liars.

And whenever our wives were away and Carlos and I were left alone together, we had sex. Again, we were having the kind of affair that many wouldn't call sex because there was never any penetration. But we satisfied each other through mutual masturbation. To others that may not have been enough. But for me and Carlos, it was all we needed to maintain the deep feelings that were developing between us.

I had arranged it so that Carlos and I lived close to each other. Brenda's and my house was just two blocks away from his. That made our relationship even more perfect because even though there were times when Carlos and I couldn't be together physically, we saw each other just about every day. Whenever he could, on his way to work, Carlos made some excuse to stop by my house. And then, the two of us would share a morning kiss.

"I love you, Jimmy," he told me each time as his wife and son waited in the car. After we shared our good morning kiss, he would run back to his car to head to work. And, I would get back into my bed with my wife with a smile on my face.

Living in San Antonio was good and it wasn't just because I had my man close. I really liked the life that I was building. It was wonderful being married to Brenda. I loved our bond. We were more than husband and wife; Brenda was truly my friend.

Between Brenda and Carlos and my precious daughter, Ebony, I felt like I was complete. And then, life became even more wonderful—Brenda became pregnant again.

This time, though, we weren't in a foreign country. So not only did we have Carlos' wife's support, but Brenda's family was able to come and visit during her pregnancy as well. That made this so much better this time around.

I couldn't imagine life being any better. I had a woman I loved, a man I loved, a daughter I loved, and now, with this pregnancy, I was praying to have a son to love.

But then, Brenda went into labor, only this time, she was way too early, months early. We called her doctor and then, I drove like a maniac, praying the entire time that our baby would be fine. At the military hospital, Brenda was rushed into a room and her doctor met us in there.

"We need to stop the contractions," the doctor told the two of us. "It's too soon for the baby to be born."

The doctor was telling us what we already knew and as I sat by Brenda's side, I prayed that God would spare and save our child. The contractions could not be stopped, though, and Brenda gave birth. But not to one child. We were shocked when she gave birth to two little boys. We had no idea that she was carrying twins.

The first of my prayers had been answered; I had not one son, but two. I was thrilled, but so scared at the same time. They didn't even weigh two pounds, and the doctor ran down all the challenges our sons had, the foremost being that their lungs were not developed; they could not breathe on their own.

As they rushed our sons into the NICU, Brenda and I held hands and prayed. But our sons were not on this earth very long. Within an hour, they had both died, born too premature to survive.

Brenda stayed in the hospital that night and so, I drove home alone, feeling as if God had forsaken me. It was difficult to maneuver the car through the tears that clouded my eyes. It was difficult to think about anything beyond the anger I had with God.

"How could you give me *two* sons and then take them away?" I cried out. "I am so mad at You!"

I told God everything that was on my heart. How I was angry. How I thought He was mean. How I'd always wanted a son and how He had doubled my pain by taking away both babies. How He didn't even give me a day to love them. I told God that He had put too much on me to bear. This was more than I could handle.

And then just as I pulled my car in front of our house and parked, God spoke to me. His words were soft, but I'm telling you, His words were audible. I truly heard the voice of God.

I had to take them. They were not ready and you were not ready for what they would have brought into your life if I had let them live.

Even though I knew the words were from God, they still hurt. And then, The Lord added, *But, I will bless you with a son.*

Maybe it was because I needed to, but I believed God. And those words gave me peace.

Still, it was not easy. Though we were surrounded by the friends that we'd made in San Antonio, especially Carlos and his wife, Brenda and I really missed our families as we grieved. Of course, our parents constantly called, checking on Brenda, checking on me, giving us their love and support.

"Bring our grandbabies home," both my mother and Brenda's mother told us. "We want them buried here near us."

We agreed. We wanted to take our sons home. But there were things that we had to take care of before we could go home and as we made plans, those few days passed slowly, feeling more like months.

It was a hard, hard time. I was concerned about Brenda, both physically and emotionally. I couldn't imagine what it was like to carry those babies for all of those months and not have them live.

While I was worried about Brenda, she was worried about me. And the two of us hardly wanted to be out of the other's sight. This tragedy pulled us even closer to each other, and closer to God. We prayed constantly and I held onto the promise that God had given me that I would have my son.

Days later, we were able to fly our sons, Ebon James and Jelani Akil back to Springfield. We had a small service at our church, complete with one small white casket that held our sons together. All during the service, all I could do was hold Brenda's hand and stare at the casket. I wasn't angry anymore, not like I'd been when we first lost our boys. But I did have lots of questions. As I listened to the preacher, I sat there and wondered what would my sons have been like? How would I have been as their father? Would we have had a better relationship than the one I had with my father? I certainly hoped so.

I never took my eyes away from the tomb that held my little boys and to this day, the picture of that tiny casket is forever branded in my mind. Our sons were buried in Ferncliff, Springfield's largest historic cemetery and I had such a hard time saying goodbye.

A few days later, we returned to San Antonio and slowly, our lives resumed, including my relationship with Carlos. But thoughts of my sons were never far from my mind and within a few months, Brenda was pregnant again. I was not surprised. Nor was I surprised when nine months later, she gave birth to our son, James Brandon. God had spoken to me; He'd given me a promise. And I knew He would do what He promised to do.

This time, our son was healthy, a nine-pound baby who was fat and happy and looked just like his deceased brothers. All I could do was smile at the gift God had given us. I felt like James was himself and the twins in one body. To this day, he is still our very special son who helped me and Brenda not to forget, but to move on.

Even though I'd been in church all of my life, I felt like that was my first personal experience with God. I felt like I really got to know Him through that tragedy. Really got to know that He really speaks to us and He keeps His word. I was so grateful that God had fulfilled His promise, but that would not be my last encounter with God. There would be another time when I would have a visitation from the Holy Spirit that would change my life.

CHAPTER 9

Back Home

*B*renda wanted to go back to Springfield and though that meant that my relationship with Carlos would have to end, I was ready to go home, too. Although I told Carlos that I would always love him and we would stay in touch, after the loss of my sons, I felt my life going in a different direction. I was closer to God, closer to my wife; this was the time for my relationship with Carlos to end.

So in 1979, I got out of the USAF. Our families had been waiting for us to return, and now that we had two children, our parents were even more anxious for us to come back to Ohio.

We returned home almost as heroes, and I got a job as a Human Resources Manager at International Harvester. Back then, IH was the biggest employer in Springfield; but although they employed hundreds of black people, I was the first black male to work in a managerial position.

Once I got that job, Brenda and I bought our first home. The four-bedroom, three bath, two-story brick home was spacious and so special to us. It was the home that we'd each dreamed of having and now, here we were, back in Springfield, among those who loved us. We were so proud of our lives and our two children, and what we'd accomplished.

At church, Brenda and I were the hot new couple, young and successful with two amazing children. We got involved with the youth ministries; I started a young adult usher board and Brenda worked in Sunday School. We were living the God-fearing, wonderful middle class life that I'd always hoped I'd have.

About a year after Brenda and I returned home, we were at church one Sunday when Deacon Melvin Gregory approached me about doing a mentoring program with him. Now, I'd known Deacon Gregory since I'd returned to Ohio; he worked at IH as well, and not too long after Brenda and I started attending that church, Deacon Gregory seemed to take a special interest in me. That didn't seem so strange, though. His interest in me was paternal. After all, he was 68 and I was 27.

Melvin Gregory was an elegant, sophisticated man who loved Billie Holiday and Ella Fitzgerald. He was really cool, single (he was divorced) and had a string of lady friends. And not only was he very respected in church (besides being a deacon, he was in the Men's choir and a member of the Senior Men's Group) but he had that same esteem in the community as well.

So whenever he asked how things were going with me, it seemed natural—like he was just looking out for a young brother. I welcomed his interest because remember, I never had that kind of relationship with my father. So, I was happy to have the deacon as a friend. One of the most important men in our church was paying attention to me. Whenever I wanted to talk, Deacon Gregory was there and not just for me; Brenda respected him, too.

When he asked me to help him get a men's mentoring program started at church, I was flattered. The deacon had chosen *me!*

"Why don't you stop by my house this Saturday so that we can talk about how to get the mentoring program started."

"Sounds good to me," I told him.

So that Saturday, I biked over to his house. It was a hot summer day and when I got there, he invited me inside and told me to relax.

"Have a seat," he said, directing me into the living room. "Do you want something to drink?"

Even though Deacon Gregory's house was only a few blocks from ours, that bike ride in that heat had really done me in and I needed that drink.

"Yes, Sir," I said, thinking that he would come back with water or if I were really lucky, maybe some lemonade.

When he returned with a bottle of E&J, an inexpensive brandy, I was surprised. But, I took the drink anyway.

"So, you wanted to talk about the mentoring program?" I asked.

"Yeah."

We talked for a few minutes, but even though we were talking about the church program, I felt a different kind of vibe from Melvin than what I was used to. It was the way he looked at me, a look that I recognized right away. I'd given that look to so many men myself.

But this was the deacon of my church! A man who knew my wife and a man whom she respected. I had to be wrong. Maybe I just had those thoughts in my head because a whole year had passed since I'd been with a guy in any way. Maybe that was why I was seeing something that wasn't there.

So, I just continued to just sit there and we talked and drank more E&J.

After about thirty minutes, the conversation shifted. When he asked me, "Do you like videos?" I knew that I hadn't imagined a thing. I'd been right about Melvin and the looks that were passing between us.

"Yeah," I told him, getting a little excited. I still wasn't sure how far he was going to take this. It was still in my mind that he was a deacon.

"Great. Why don't you come upstairs? There are some videos I want to show you."

I followed him. I had done this before; I knew what was going to happen. There would be some bumping and grinding, maybe some oral sex. And I was turned on by that.

To be honest, I'd been fighting my feelings since I'd left San Antonio. I wanted to have a normal life with my wife and children, but inside, something still stirred when I saw a good-looking man. My hope was that whatever was going to happen with the deacon would be enough to give me the release that I needed, and then, I would be able to go back to my life.

Inside his bedroom, he motioned for me to sit on his bed before he turned to a stack of video cassettes on the shelf. When he popped the first one in, images of naked men filled the TV screen.

At this point, I was E&J'd out, the scene on TV was turning me on even more, and I kept thinking that it had been so long. So when Deacon Gregory laid down next to me, I was ready. But what I wasn't ready for was everything that the deacon had in mind.

It started off "innocently" enough; Melvin kissed my neck and I became even more aroused. Then, he took it further. First, he undressed me, before he did the same. I'd never been completely naked with a man before. And without even exchanging a single word, we had sex.

I mean, we really had sex. None of that foreplay stuff that I was used to doing. We had sex—from oral to penetration, we did it all. We did the things that I'd been dreaming about all of my life. We did all of those things...and he satisfied me. Deacon Melvin Gregory turned me out.

When I left Melvin's home several hours later, I knew that he had awakened something in me that I'd never thought would ever fully take bloom. Yes, I had done other things, but now I knew that was all child's play. This was the real deal and I loved it.

After that, I couldn't get enough of Melvin. He satisfied every sexual desire within me. He touched me in ways that I hadn't been touched before. It was like he knew what I needed before I knew it myself. He fulfilled desires that I didn't even know I had.

Looking back, I can see that Melvin's seduction began on the day that Brenda and I entered our church. But I didn't see it. It was the perfect seduction and as the weeks and months passed, the deacon and I became closer.

And now, the perfect seduction had become the perfect affair. Think about it—Melvin lived nearby, he was very respected, Brenda liked him. And he was a deacon in our church!

But what was most important about him at that point—Melvin was my lover who taught me how to love a man.

My world was great. With my wife, my children, my job... and Melvin, I had everything that I wanted. It is important for you to understand that my being with Melvin had nothing to do with Brenda. She was still the perfect wife, still supportive of me in every way and I still felt so blessed to have her.

It was just that with Melvin, I didn't have to be the man all the time. With Melvin, I could be myself, I could let my guard down, be authentic, be who I truly was. With Melvin every one of those desires that had always been inside of me were freed. I could breathe. I was receiving a love that Brenda could never give to me, no matter how hard she tried.

It was about far more than sex with Melvin. I was able to talk to him about anything, the type of things that I would have loved to share with my father. And Melvin seemed to have all the answers. Remember, he was forty years older and I appreciated and needed his wisdom.

He was a great friend, a master teacher sexually, and always emotionally supportive. But he also had his PhD in living on the down low. He knew what to do, what to say. He knew how to keep our lives a secret...and he taught me how to do the same. It was wonderful. I thought we'd go on like that forever.

The challenge, though, was that the closer I became with Melvin, the more distance I put between me and Brenda. Of course, our sex life changed and Brenda began to wonder what was going on. When she asked me why I wasn't as affectionate as I used to be, I told her it was because I was stressed adjusting to life as a civilian. When she asked me why I spent so much time away from home, I told her that we'd been away for a long time and there were people I had to see. Plus, I'd started taking classes at a local college. I wasn't interested in anything in particular, I was just taking advantage of the VA bill.

Brenda accepted my responses because she trusted me. Not that she was naive. It was just that I'd earned her trust and had never given her a single reason not to trust me. And so, she did...or so, I thought. I took her understanding and kindness as an opportunity to do whatever I wanted. I took her not questioning me too much as a sign of her belief and faith in me.

I got comfortable. I got cocky. I got careless.

When visiting Melvin, I parked my car right in front of his house, not once, but many times. I guess it happened one too many times, though, because one of Brenda's friends spotted my car and called my wife. Later, I found out that she'd told Brenda that it wasn't the first time I'd been at Melvin's for hours.

That night when I came home, Brenda never let on what she knew. Instead, she asked me what she always did.

"How was your day?"

"It was okay," I said. "I was in class."

That's what I told Brenda, but I had given up those classes weeks ago, so that I could spend all of my "school time" with Melvin. I continued my lie with, "Class was tough, too. The professor was on me the entire time."

With those words, I was busted big time and didn't even know it. All of the suspicions that had been hovering inside of Brenda meshed together and she went into detective mode.

The next day when I went to Melvin's house, the same way I'd been going for months, Brenda drove over right behind me.

Of course, my gold Cutlass was in the driveway. And in the small town we lived in, it was not unusual for people to leave the doors unlocked, at least not in the 70s. So Brenda opened that front door, heard the music blasting from Melvin's bedroom, walked up the stairs, and saw me and Melvin together on his bed. He and I were so caught up that we never noticed her.

Now, I've never been sure exactly what Brenda saw. All I know is that she saw enough to be disgusted. She saw enough to know for sure that our marriage was over. Without saying a word, she rushed out of that house.

When I got home just a few hours later, having been satisfied by Melvin and now looking forward to spending the evening with my wife and children, my key wouldn't fit into the front door lock. I kept trying to twist it and finally, I had to ring the doorbell.

My wife's youngest brother answered the door.

"Hey...."

Before I could get any more words out, he stepped to me, got in my face and said, "You better get your faggot ass out of here before I fuck you up!"

My heart started beating like a drum. *What was going on?*

"John...." I said to him.

But even as I tried to step around him, he blocked my path. Over his shoulder, I saw Brenda at the kitchen table sobbing, and surrounded by the rest of her siblings.

"Get away from here, man!" John shouted.

I backed up only because there were more of them than me. But the whole time I was trying to figure out, what the hell happened? As I got into my car and backed out of the driveway, I quickly scrolled through my day. Of course I knew what I'd done, but there was no way that Brenda could have found out about that. How could she?

At first, all I wanted to do was go back to Melvin's house. He would help me figure this out. But, I was smart enough not to do that. I didn't go there. In fact, though I didn't know it then, I would never step foot inside Melvin's house again.

But there was little solace at my parents' home. Brenda had called them, told them what happened and how we were getting a divorce because she'd caught me having sex with a man.

When my father said, "How could you do this to us? How could you embarrass your family this way? How am I going to face everyone at church?" that was the moment when I knew for sure Brenda had somehow found out about me and Melvin.

While my father was pissed, my mother was heartbroken. She cried and I cried with her. But even as I cried into my mother's chest, I prayed that I would somehow be able to put my family back together. I prayed that Brenda would forgive me.

But it was not to be. No matter what I tried to do, no matter how much I told Brenda that I loved her, how much I promised that what she saw with me and Melvin would never happen again, Brenda would not take me back. I had one strike and I was out.

Without my wife and children, I went into a deep depression. I stopped eating and could hardly sleep. I missed Brenda so much, but I'd hurt her so deeply, there was no coming back.

Three months after Brenda found me in bed with a man, I was served with divorce papers. My marriage was over and that began a new downward spiral in my life.

CHAPTER 10

Finding Love or Sex or Me

*A*fter the divorce was final, I had to leave Springfield. The city was too small and it was the kind of place where everyone knew everybody's business. So of course, I was the talk of the city. Everybody was talking about Jimmy King and how he disgraced his family. How he was caught with one of the old men from St. John's Missionary Baptist Church. How Brenda had caught him and now he was back, living at home with his parents, and depressed.

But it was more than people outside my home that drove me out of Springfield. It was what was happening inside my parents' home. Like I said before, I'd never connected emotionally with my dad, but I could read his emotions now. He was so angry that he could hardly look at me. And the times when I did catch him staring at me, I was convinced that there was nothing but hate in his eyes.

Though my mother was upset, she did all that she could to help, but nothing she could do would take away the pain.

That's what hurt her the most. My hurt—even though deep down she was glad to have me home, she hurt because I hurt.

But though I was so grateful for my mother's unconditional love, it wasn't enough to keep me there. I was only twenty-seven and the first in my family to be divorced. In my family, in that little town, divorce carried almost as much of a stigma as what I'd been caught doing with Melvin.

Then, as if I was being punished for my crimes, I was laid off from my job. And the home that Brenda and I had purchased together went into foreclosure. My life was so dark, there was no choice. I had to get away.

So, I packed my bags and headed to Columbus, Ohio. Why Columbus? Because I knew a few people there and it was far enough away, yet close enough. I didn't have a job, I didn't even have any prospects, but I was determined to make something happen in Columbus.

After just a few days of being there, I felt like I'd moved into a brave new world. Without a wife, I didn't have to be sneaky and I went buckwild. I found brothers who could meet my sexual needs. I found brothers who could fulfill me the way Melvin had.

But the sad part was that I hadn't learned any lessons from what I'd just gone through. Because instead of just being with men, I started dating women, too.

Yes, I'd been caught by my wife, but it wasn't like I was gay. I was determined to be "normal." I wanted a straight life with a wonderful woman where I would just have men on the side.

So I ended up dragging another young lady into my web of lies and deception.

This time, it was Kim. Kim was a fine sister who lived in a city about thirty miles from Columbus. She was a nurse, and a single mother of three daughters. Honestly, I didn't have to do much to get her; all I had to do was turn on my charm and sex appeal and she fell in love. Not too much time passed before I moved in with her and her daughters.

That was a relief for me. I still hadn't found a job and my funds were low, so I was willing to exchange great sex for room and board. And I really laid it down when it came to sex, sexing her so good that if anyone ever told her that I was gay, there was no way that she would believe it. If anyone ever told her that I'd just been caught in bed with another man and had lost my wife and family from my secretive behavior, she would have called that person a straight-out liar.

You see, besides being an attentive and satisfying sexual partner, Kim thought I was the most honest man she'd ever met. When she asked me if I'd ever been married, I didn't lie about that...I told her yes. And I told her that our divorce was my fault; I'd hurt my wife.

That was way before Google, so she appreciated my truthfulness. And because she trusted me from just that one little question, she gave me everything: her mind, her body, and her soul. She did everything for me: she cooked (and she could cook her butt off), paid my bills and met any other need that I had. She helped me through the freshness of my divorce and without even knowing it, played into helping me fool myself. She helped me believe that I was "holding onto my straightness."

Truly, I appreciated her and tried to be the best man she'd ever been with. But in reality I just used her. I needed a woman who would take care of me, who could cover for me, especially a woman that I could take home to my parents and Kim was perfect for that role.

I'd done such a good job of keeping my secrets from her, but like everything that's done in the dark, it always comes to light.

I'd only been living with Kim a short time when she introduced me to Andrew, a young man who was a friend of one of her brothers. It didn't take long for me and Andrew to end up in bed together. And what was so bad—we used her bed in her home.

Kim worked the third shift and right after she pulled out of the garage at 11PM, Andrew would pull right into the driveway. He would stay there all night with me, sleeping in her bed, leaving just a little before she came home at seven in the morning.

Andrew became my habit, and I guess, some habits are hard to break. And so, of course Kim found out. With just a little bit of snooping she found the evidence that Andrew and

I had left behind on paper—cards, love letters. And then, she found the videos.

The videos were the things that would get me in trouble all the time!

So that ended my relationship with Kim. Now, I had to find someone new. Someone who could help take care of me because clearly, I couldn't take care of myself. I was just going to have to be more careful the next time.

CHAPTER 11

On My Own

*I*t was hard being on my own. Think about it; I had gone from my parents' home into the military and then straight into a life with Brenda. And for the last few months, I'd been taken care of by Kim.

So this being truly alone and completely on my own was a first. I may have been twenty-seven, but it was a struggle because I still didn't have a job. And, I started being really depressed about that.

To take my mind off of being by myself, I started hanging out with the few gay friends that I knew in Columbus. Just about every weekend, I'd hang out at parties, mostly house parties and it was a good distraction. I'd meet guys, hang out a little, but it was at one of these parties, where I met this really nice, really good looking brother.

I was standing alone, sipping on a drink when he walked up to me.

"I'm Gilbert," he said, holding out his hand.

"I'm Jim."

That was the beginning of an all-night conversation that led to a few dates and ended up with me moving in with him. Yes, it was fast, but I had to move quickly since I didn't have any money. After Kim, I was just moving from one friend's couch to another. So having one place to stay felt like a blessing to me.

Not even a year had passed since my divorce, and I was with my first live-in male lover. I was ambivalent about it. I mean, I think I liked being with Gilbert, but what I liked most about our relationship was that I needed someone to take care of me. And Gilbert did that. He cooked, he took care of his home...he did everything that a wife would do. And that's what I needed—a wife. I made that man my wife.

Beyond his 'wifely' duties, Gilbert took care of me financially, too. He made pretty good money as the manager of one of the larger Kroger stores in the city. So, he covered all of my bills, including paying my child support.

I didn't know anything about being with a man or being in the gay life, so I never planned to get too settled into it. To me, I was still straight and just kicking it with guys. And it was very comfortable kicking it with Gilbert.

We even went to church every Sunday as a couple, though we were on the DL, of course. To our church members, we were just two single men, men who were friends, who came to worship the Lord together.

Church wasn't the only place where we kept our relationship to ourselves. Gilbert wasn't out to anyone, not his family, not his friends or co-workers and he took great care in hiding me. We lived together in a one-bedroom apartment, so we hardly had any visitors because that would have certainly given our situation away. However, when any of his family members did come to visit, we made sure that I was out of the house.

But it wasn't just his friends and family that made it a challenge for us. Living with Gilbert made it really difficult for me to be a father. I wanted to spend the weekends with my children, but I couldn't bring them to Columbus and have them see me in a one-bedroom with a dude. That would be all that Brenda needed to make sure that they never came to stay with me. So for a while, my children didn't visit me at all.

Talk about being depressed. Being away from my children was the hardest of all. I loved my son and daughter and wanted to spend time with them. But without working, I didn't have any money to feed myself, let alone feed them or take them someplace else to stay for a couple of nights. I wouldn't even have been able to take them to McDonald's if they had come for a visit.

There was nothing I could do about it. It wasn't like I had a big choice about my living arrangements and my relationship. I would have been homeless without Gilbert. So whether I liked it or not, I learned how to be Gilbert's man.

Gilbert and I never missed church on Sunday and one day after services, one of the assistant pastors came over to us.

"Do you guys have a moment?" he asked.

"Sure," we said together.

He got straight to the point. "I'm forming a new ministry for singles to mix and mingle. I want to plan a few get-togethers and maybe even go on trips. We want to connect the single Christians, so maybe one day they'll get married." He paused. "So, what do you think?"

I could feel Gilbert looking at me, but I kept my eyes on the minister. "Great!" I said.

He smiled. "Well, I'm glad to hear that 'cause I want the two of you there. You're two of the church's most handsome and eligible single brothers. The sisters have been checking you both out."

He laughed and I did, too. Gilbert didn't.

The minister finished up with, "So, can I count on you?"

"Sure," I answered once again for the both of us.

The minister didn't seem to notice that I was the only one talking. "Great. We have a meeting coming up next Wednesday after Bible Study. It's at 8:30pm in the fellowship hall. Will you be able to be there?"

"I will," I said eagerly.

And Gilbert told him he'd be there, too.

I didn't know about Gilbert, but I was excited. All of those single women? I knew how to use what I had to get what I wanted. And with the right amount of swagger, I just might be able to find a woman who would love me and want to take care of me. With any luck, I'd find a female live-in lover.

You see, even though Gilbert had been good to me, I had to get out. I didn't need to be living with a man, I needed to be with a woman. And this ministry was going to be the perfect opportunity, this was going to be my perfect out. I'd meet a woman and not just any ordinary woman. I was going to meet a church girl that I could take home to my parents. Then maybe I wouldn't have to see that disgusted glare on my father's face, or the worry in my mother's eyes anymore. And then, Brenda would hear the news about my new woman and my ex-wife would see that I did love women. And I wasn't gay. And maybe she'd even regret not taking me back.

The more I thought about it, the more I liked the idea. I even began to think about meeting the right lady and getting married once again. That seemed logical and possible to me... after all, I was still a man.

On the way home, I passed my idea past Gilbert...sort of.

"I think Minister Williams had a good idea about the single's ministry."

"Yeah," Gilbert grumbled.

When he didn't add anything else, I said, "I think when that group meets, we need to be there and hook up with some women. Find girlfriends."

"What?" The way he said it, I could tell he was upset already. I guess he knew what I was thinking before I said it.

"Look," I began, "I think we spend too much time together and soon people will be looking at us suspiciously if they're not already. Especially in our apartment building and at church."

"I don't know about where we live, but no one is suspicious at church. Minister Williams just told us that women have been asking about us."

"That's what I'm saying," I said. "We have a chance to make sure we don't have any issues."

I kept saying that we needed cover girls and he kept saying that we didn't. But I was the man in our relationship and what I said was the law for the most part.

Gilbert was quiet for the rest of the way home and even once we arrived at our apartment, he had very little to say.

But I knew exactly what to do to get him on my side. I did what I'd become so good at doing—I used sex to get what I wanted. I sexed him real good, gave him good loving, and before the night was over, he agreed with me.

"You're right," he said as we laid together in bed.

So we made plans on how we would meet the perfect sisters to date. We'd go out, even take them to church with us.

"But promise me that this is just for a cover," he said.

"What do you mean?"

"We should make a promise that we won't ever have sex with them, we won't fall in love, and we will never let a woman come between us."

"I promise," I said, and sealed my words with a kiss.

But inside, I knew that I was looking for a wife. What I needed was an out from this gay shit.

There were so many reasons why I had to get out. First, I wasn't going to hell with Gilbert and secondly, I was not ever going to let my children see their dad in a homosexual relationship.

But, I wasn't going to let on about what I was really thinking. I was going to play Gilbert, and play the sisters at the same time. This was all about getting everything that I had to get.

And at this time what I had to get was a good woman.

CHAPTER 12

Cover Girls

We'd found what we were looking for. Shelia and her roommate and best friend, Wendy were the perfect cover girls. Especially since we met them at church.

Gilbert and I had gone to a couple of those single programs that Minister Williams had started, but to no avail. And then one Sunday, when the pastor asked for guests to stand, these two sisters stood up and I knew they were the ones. Gilbert didn't seem to notice them and even if he had, I knew in his heart he was still against what I wanted to do. But what he wanted didn't matter.

After church, we walked up to the two of them, welcomed them to the church and after just chatting for a little while, I could tell they were as attracted to us as I was to them. (Gilbert, of course, still wasn't interested.)

After a couple of more meetings at church and a couple of church programs, we paired off. My man was more into Wendy because I told him he would be, and because I wanted Sheila to be my girl. She was a gorgeous woman: light-skinned, with green eyes, and long flowing natural hair. But not only did she look good, she had everything else going for her, too. She and Wendy shared a luxury apartment not too far from downtown Columbus and she worked as an insurance claims adjuster making six figures. She had no kids, was from a small town in southern Ohio...yup, Sheila was the perfect woman for me. She would make my parents real happy and she would make me look good. Together, we were a great-looking couple.

While Sheila loved to get out and have some fun, Wendy was a bit more reserved. Raised in the COGIC, she was all about her faith and going to church all day on Sunday, then back again on Monday, Tuesday, Wednesday, Thursday, Friday, and Saturday.

She was nice looking, too. A tall dark-skinned sister who could have easily been a model, Wendy was also in insurance; she was a very successful agent. So those two best friends became involved with these two best friends—at least that's what we told them. That Gilbert and I were best friends.

The four of us were striking together when we strutted into church, all of us sharp, looking like a million dollars. We walked in and heads turned.

And we turned heads outside of church, too. Everywhere we went, people looked at us. And everywhere we went, we went together. From dinner to dancing, it was me and Sheila, Gilbert and Wendy.

I was having a great time being in a relationship with Gilbert and Sheila. There was that little thing that we had to explain, though...the fact that Gilbert and I were living together in a one-bedroom apartment. But it was an easy enough lie to tell.

"I just moved here from Springfield and haven't found a job yet. So, my boy Gilbert, who I've known since school, was kind enough to let me sleep on his couch."

It seemed logical to the girls and I'd become so adept at lying that I almost believed what I said.

The more time we spent together, the more our relationship progressed, it was good for me and Gilbert, but apparently not for the girls. They started getting antsy. They were fine with us all being friends and everything, but they wanted more individual time with their new boos.

"Why do we always have to do things with Gilbert and Wendy?" Sheila would whine. "Why can it just be you and me?"

I was always somehow able to side-step her request, but I had to handle Gilbert. He didn't always act right when it came to Sheila. When she dropped by to see me or brought me gifts, Gilbert got pissed. And Sheila noticed it.

"You know, sometimes he acts like he's your woman," she said, shaking her head. "He gets such an attitude when I come by."

"Really? You're imaging that," I would tell her. "And you know I love you, right?"

That was all I had to say. I used my skills to keep her clueless. But it wasn't easy because Gilbert *did* act like a pissed-off bitch. He hated when she did anything for me and we'd argue about it after she left. I was able to keep him in check, though. But juggling a woman and a man was a life full of lies and a full-time job.

I handled it, though. I continued to date Shelia and my man continued to date Wendy. The holidays came and I took Sheila home to meet my parents and my kids. Everyone loved her. My father didn't look at me with so much disdain and the stress lines were gone from my mother's face.

And my kids liked her so much, they didn't mind sharing her with me during their weekend visits. I was able to bring them to Columbus now since Sheila paid for everything that I needed to make their time with us great. We'd stay in a hotel and even though the kids were there, Sheila felt like she had some alone time with me, away from Gilbert and Wendy. It worked because my children always looked forward to seeing her.

Everything was going well until....

One day Sheila was over. She surprised me while Gilbert was at work and I was actually glad to see her. I wasn't expecting her, so I went out to pick up a pizza for us to eat.

"I'm going to lay down while I wait for you," she told me.

"Okay, I'll be right back."

Now, I should have known better because I'd learned enough by this time to know that women are born investigators, or another way to put it—they are nosey! So while she was in my bedroom—only God knows how it actually went down, but I later found out that she first found our videos, the hardcore videos of men having sex.

From there, I can only imagine what she did. She went through my nightstand, I know that because she found the letter, along with condoms and lub. But it was the letter that was the most damaging. The letter from my man telling me how much he loved me and wanted to be with me for the rest of our lives. It was a letter that obviously wasn't meant for Sheila's eyes—especially since he wrote about her! He said that he was sick and tired of Shelia taking time away from him. And then, he went on to graphically say that though he didn't like Sheila being around, that he did enjoy sucking my dick every time she left, knowing that was something that she would never be able to do for me.

When I returned home with the large veggie pizza and a bottle of wine, Sheila met me at the door. She was a complete mess with smudged mascara blackening her red eyes.

She didn't even have to say anything; I knew what had happened. Not specifically, but I knew I was busted. I expected her to start swinging, to start calling me every name in the my-man-is-a-cheater book. But she wasn't the angry black woman, not at all.

Instead, with tears streaming down her face, she softly asked, "Why didn't you tell me you were gay?" She paused as she sobbed. "Why didn't you tell me that you and Gilbert were lovers?"

I stood there, trying to think of something to say, but I didn't say a word. And I wondered, how many times was I going to do this to women? First it was Brenda, and then, Kim, and now Sheila.

She asked, "Why did you lie to me? I loved you, I gave you all of me."

That was when I noticed the letter she held. She brought it up to my eye-level and asked, "Is this true? Is what he wrote true?"

I shook my head. For anyone else, the jig would've been up. But for me...I wasn't going to give up that easily. So I reached out to her and was surprised when she actually let me lead her to the living room couch.

When we sat down, she repeated, "Is this true?"

Looking into her eyes, I forced a tear from my eye and let it drip down my cheek. "No," I said, still shaking my head. "Gilbert wants to be with me, but I won't give in. No, there's nothing between us."

She frowned as if that was the last answer she expected. "Then why...."

I didn't even let her finish her question. "Let me explain," I said. "Gilbert has always wanted to be with me, but to me, he's just my best friend. He won't stop, though. He keeps trying to get me with those letters." I pointed to the one she held. "He writes me that stuff all the time, but it's nothing but his fantasy."

The way she looked at me, I could see that she wanted to believe me, but had her doubts.

I turned it up, putting on the performance of my life. "You know me, Sheila. You've been around me. You know I'm not gay."

She was quiet as if in her mind, she was rolling through all the times we'd been together. I knew what her gut was telling her. That's why I had to go for her heart. I grabbed her hand. "This is what we need to do," I said. "You and I need to pray for Gilbert and ask God to release him from the demon spirit of homosexuality that has taken over his body and his mind." Then, as the final act, I collapsed against her, falling into her chest. "Just hold me, Sheila. Please hold me. I don't know why Gilbert would want me. It's been so confusing. But if we pray... if the two of us really pray, God will help him, God will heal him."

As she put her arms around me, I knew Sheila was smart. She knew the truth, but her heart wouldn't let her listen to her head. Like so many women before her, like so many women who can't (or don't want to) face their own intuition, she bought my story.

"Okay," she said softly, rubbing my back. "We'll pray for Gilbert."

"Thank you," I said, rising up and looking into her eyes.

"But...."

Uh-oh. I didn't know what was coming.

"We have to find you an apartment as soon as possible. You can't stay here!"

"You're right," I said. "I can't stay here."

It was an Oscar worthy performance and I'd thrown my man under the bus. I had to because I wanted to keep Sheila in my life.

That night though, Sheila left the moment Gilbert got home. It was as if she couldn't stand to look at him. "Are you going to be all right staying here?" she whispered when I walked her to the door.

"Of course. I've been here all this time and nothing has happened. And nothing is going to happen. You can believe that. I'm not gay."

She smiled and I gave her a peck on her lips.

When I turned back into my apartment, Gilbert said, "What's wrong with Sheila."

"Man, she found everything!"

"What?"

I told him how she'd gone snooping through my room.

"And she still wants to be with you?"

"Hell, yeah!" I said, and then explained what I'd done.

When I finished, Gilbert laughed. "Really? She believed that?"

"She bought the whole story," I said, then laughed with him.

It was the biggest turn on. For both of us. Because that night we had some of the hottest, wildest sex.

A few months later, I did finally end it with Sheila. But all I did was move on from her to some other woman. I didn't change my ways. I didn't change my bad behavior or habits or lying. For years, I just kept using men and women to my advantage. It was as if after I lost Brenda, I lost my mind. I couldn't find it in my heart to care about anyone. So, I focused only on me; I cared only about me.

I continued to lie, to cheat, and really even steal because lying and cheating got me things from men and women that they wouldn't have given me if they'd known the truth.

I was the King of Deception, and on the outside, I was proud of it. I say on the outside because when I laid down at night, and put my head on that pillow, I always wondered what I was doing. And, I knew I needed to stop.

But I didn't stop. The lies continued, the deception kept on. Of course, that finally led me to break up with Gilbert, too. I left after he found out that I was cheating on him. It was no big deal to me; he was never going to be my forever man.

So, I moved on. The thing is, though, you can't keep messing over people and not expect it to boomerang back to you. There is a price you're going to have to pay, a price with God and a price with man. It was going to happen one day. And my one day came in many different ways.

CHAPTER 13

The Lost Years

I had lost my mind. Seriously, that's how I felt. Maybe it was because losing my wife, and feeling like I'd lost my children was harder on me than I wanted to admit. I did see a therapist for a while, to talk about how I was still hurting even though my divorce was more than a year behind me.

To mask my pain, I did whatever I wanted to do. I got heavy into the sex party scene. Now, if you've never heard of sex parties, these are popular parties where lots of men pay a fee to attend. In other words it's a pay-to-be-there orgy. It can be a big event, with hundreds of men, or small, private parties. It never mattered to me. I spent weekend after weekend at these parties drinking alcohol, using drugs, and having lots of sex with freaky, naked men.

And then, there were those Internet sites. Man, that was like a kid going to a candy store. On the sites the men were on display and I could pick anything I wanted. It was like a buffet—a spread of men where I could have any kind of man:

married, straight, all shapes and sizes. All I had to do was click on a picture and make a phone call.

But my life wasn't just about men. Men were for sex and I really wanted a relationship. So, I moved from woman to woman, always looking for someone to take care of me, always looking for that woman that I could one day marry, and always ending up getting kicked out once the woman found out that I was a liar and a cheater.

There were so many men, so many women that I lost count and lost track of the names. That's why I refer to that time as the lost years. I was lost and even now, I have a hard time remembering all the things that happened to me during those two decades in Columbus.

But though I don't remember much, there are a couple of life-changing situations that I will never be able to forget.

I said that I didn't remember names, but there was this one man during that time...Carl Cunningham. He was one man who was hard to forget. He was young, and fine...and a pastor. Yes, he was the new pastor at one of the most popular churches in Columbus and from the moment he arrived (he was from West Virginia) he was the star of Columbus. Everybody wanted this man and everybody got him. Men and women—it didn't matter. In less than a month, he became known as the whore of Columbus. But nobody seemed to care about that. Nobody seemed to care that Pastor Cunningham was screwing anything that wasn't nailed down. He was just that fine.

And the person who seemed to care the least was his wife!

Yup, the pastor was married. There was no way that she didn't know what was going on. She had to know, everyone else did. But she stayed. And every Sunday, she sat in that front pew with a smile on her face like the good First Lady that she was as Pastor Cunningham delivered his message from the pulpit.

Clearly during this time, I wasn't being spiritually fed, though Pastor Cunningham definitely satisfied my sexual appetite.

It was a crazy time, but that's just how it was during those lost years. I wasn't the only one who was lost. It was all about having a good time, even though we were all reckless. We were reckless not only because we were sexing everyone, but we were having unprotected sex. HIV and AIDs just didn't seem important. It certainly wasn't going to affect any of us...until it did.

Pastor Cunningham left about two years after he got there. We all thought that he'd been moved to another church because of all the rumors about his sexual escapades. But a few years after that, we found out the real reason for his sudden departure. Pastor Cunningham had passed away. He died from AIDS.

When I got that call, it knocked the wind of me. I'm not kidding. I passed out on my bed and then when I woke up, I was consumed with thoughts about Pastor Cunningham. He had actually died? Of AIDS?

All I could do was sit in my apartment and think about all the unprotected sex I'd had with him. And when my girlfriend came home, all I could think about was the unprotected sex I'd had with her right after having unprotected sex with him.

For the first time since I'd started living in this lifestyle, I was scared. This news felt like a death sentence to me. Would I live to see next year? Of course, I had to get tested, even though I didn't want to. I was too scared of what the test would tell me. But I did go in and while I waited for those results I couldn't do a thing. Back then, it took a couple of weeks to get the results, so I spent days not being able to breathe.

When the tests came back that I was negative, I praised God, knowing that it was only because of His grace that I was not only alive, but not infected either. Then, I waited to get the news from my friends who had also had Pastor Cunningham as a sexual partner. And for weeks, just about every day, I received the awful news.

Everyone that I knew who'd slept with Pastor Cunningham was infected—including his wife. And over the next couple of years, my friends died...one by one. Everybody that I knew of who'd been with the pastor died—except for me.

You know that affected me for a long, long time. But unfortunately not enough to change my behavior. In fact, I became even wilder if that were possible. I hadn't been infected. Maybe I was immune to the virus. Or maybe I just had a bigger purpose on earth and I wasn't going to die of AIDS. So to me, that gave me carte blanche to do whatever I wanted to do.

Trust me, though, I thanked God for being alive. But the next event made me question God again. I know we all have to take the same journey, but when my mother died, I couldn't understand why God would take her away from me.

It was such a shock to get that call—that my dear mother had passed away. She hadn't been sick, which I'm glad about. It was sudden and to this day, it is still so difficult for me to talk about. But there was a silver lining to me that I wouldn't see until years later. I had no idea of the turn that my life was about to take. I had no idea that I was about to become JL King. And I wouldn't have ever wanted my mother to live through that.

Still, that time was so hard for me and I think the emotional toll of losing the person who was dearest to me contributed to my downward spiral. Those lost years were like a black hole where I kept sinking deeper and deeper. I lost job after job because I kept propositioning men. But it was like I couldn't stop, or maybe it was that I didn't care.

Then, there were the women. I told lie after lie to get women to take care of me. I hurt women as if it were a sport, though truly, that was not my intention.

It was a time of peaks and valleys, a time of exhilaration and depression. But it wasn't a time of any self-awareness. I wasn't growing, I wasn't learning. I was hard headed, not gaining from life lessons that these situations gave me.

It went on that way year after year. Until God got tired of me. I'm sure that's what happened. God got sick and tired. He had put me on this earth for a purpose and I wasn't living up to it. So God had something for me. And, I'm telling you, I wasn't ready.

CHAPTER 14

Go Away God!

So now here I was, working at the Urban League. Like I said in the beginning, it was a good job, and I was grateful for running into Sam Gresham that day at the cleaners and thankful to him for pulling me out of the gutter. But I was still struggling since the job only paid $10,500 a year.

Once I got that job, though, my life began to look up. Like I'd always done, I supplemented my income by dating this fine sister who helped me out. At her suggestion, I used her credit to get an apartment, and I was even driving a brand new Mazda 626, so I thought I was the man. Everyone else thought that, too: I had a great position, looked the part of a young executive, I was back to being one of the hottest single brothers in Columbus, Ohio.

Those were all the thoughts I had one night when I was chilling in my apartment, just reflecting on my wonderful life. I loved women, had sex with men...it didn't get better than this.

I was laying in my bed, thinking about what I was going to do the next day, the next week, the next month...when all of a sudden, I became bolted down in my bed. Literally. I don't know what happened, but I could not move. It was like I'd been shackled.

I tried...I tried to move my arms, my legs, but I couldn't even turn my head. Even when I opened my mouth, not a sound came out.

I don't think I'd ever been more afraid. What was going on? Was this what happened before you died?

Then a shadow appeared at the foot of my bed. In my mind, I fought to get away, but I was rooted in place, stiff as stone. Now, I was beyond scared, terrified, really. But there was nothing I could do. My time had come, this was how I was going to die.

Tears rolled down my cheeks as I stared into the face of death. I might not have been able to move, but my mind was clear. I wondered how death was going to come. I wondered if it would hurt. I wondered where I would be going.

Then, I heard a voice. "Tell your story."

What the hell?

"Tell your story."

I waited for the voice to say more. But over and over, all it said was, "Tell your story."

Slowly, my fear began to fade as it seemed that the shadow hadn't come to escort me to the afterlife. But still, I couldn't figure any of this out. *Tell my story?* What story? I would've asked, but I still couldn't speak.

Then, the shadow disappeared, even though the words stayed. "Tell your story!"

A few seconds later, I was freed. I jumped out of the bed and fell straight to my knees. Once again, I was scared, but this time it was a different kind of fear. I knew like I knew my own name that the Spirit had come to me. But why me? And why now? And what was the story that I was supposed to tell? And who was I supposed to tell it to?

I prayed and prayed, asking God what was He saying? I still didn't have any answers when I got off the floor, but I felt such peace. A peace that I hadn't felt in a long time. Maybe that was why when the same thing happened to me the next night, and the next night, for three nights in a row, I didn't feel the fear that I'd felt at first.

Every night as I laid in bed, suddenly, I'd be frozen in place, and then seconds later, the shadow would come. And say the same words: "Tell your story."

But each time I was left with the same question—what story? And why me?

On the third night, though, the shadow said just a bit more. "Tell your story." And then, the shadow added, "Tell your story, and I will take you on a journey that will save lives. You will be both loved and hated, but you will be serving me and I will be with you. This is the purpose for your life. Trust me."

That night, when the shadow faded and I was freed, I had a feeling that that was the last time I'd have this visitation. A part of me was sad—I still didn't know what I was supposed to do. My question was still the same—what story?

The next morning, I went about my day as I always did, this time, having lunch with a very good friend. We met at Denny's, his favorite place for the Grand Slam Specials, and after we placed our orders, before we even began our normal male-chat session, my friend said to me, "Jimmy, I don't know what this means, but God told me to tell you to be obedient to what He has asked you to do."

My eyes widened and I almost fell out of my chair. My friend's words were confirmation. I'd heard God, I wasn't imagining what had been happening to me the past few nights. But at the same time that God had given me this confirmation, He also gave me clarity.

I knew what I was supposed to do! I understood—my story. He wanted me to tell the story about how I was living a life of lies and deception. He wanted me to tell how I was living in denial.

Now, I was scared for real. If that was the story that I was supposed to tell, I'd be a living sacrifice. I would be exposing myself on a very personal level. And, I'd have to expose others, too.

But then, I remembered God's words: I will be with you... this is the purpose of your life...trust Me.

I'd made a lot of mistakes in my life. I was hard-headed and at times, I could be self-centered. But even with my faults, there was one thing about me—I knew God and I loved Him. And I knew that I could trust Him.

If God said He wanted me to take this journey and if He said He was going to be with me, then this was a journey that I was willing to take. Even as scared as I was, I was going to do it.

I didn't yet know how or when, but I was going to be obedient. And so right there in Denny's my journey began.

One thing, though, I was going to tell the truth, but I had to protect my family as well as I could. And so the first thing I would need was a new name.

CHAPTER 15

I am J. Louis King

Hello. My name is J. Louis King and I have sex with men and women. I am not gay and there are thousands of men out there just like me!"

That is what I said to a room full of men and women, doctors, scientists, and HIV prevention professionals, who were all attending the Black AIDS conference in DC.

I said those words and the room fell silent.

Then, "What did he say?" one of the people in the audience shouted.

It was crazy, but I wasn't sure what I was going to say next. Four hundred people were staring at the podium where I was speaking and I didn't have a planned presentation.

Yeah, I should've been prepared, but really, I was just there for the $500.00 that I was offered. This was my first formal paid presentation, but I figured I could just wing it and say what was on my mind: I had sex with men and women and I wasn't gay and didn't like being associated with gay men and there were lots of other men like me.

With all of those eyes on me, I added, "I don't use condoms and I don't know what my HIV status is and really, I don't want to know." Then, because I didn't have anything else to say, I repeated, "I have sex with men and women, and I am not gay."

It was as if the heavens were opening (or maybe the opening was the gates of hell); the entire room exploded.

"What did he say?"

"No, he didn't."

"That nigga is crazy."

And those were only the words I understood. The room was in an uproar, there was a meltdown. The organizer of the conference center grabbed me and pulled me off stage, taking me to a room behind the stage.

"Stay in here until things calm down a bit," he told me. "I'm going to step out there and try to handle this."

I'm sure the organizer thought he'd taken me to a secure location, but only a few minutes had passed before I heard the voices. Women's voices. And I heard their questions.

"I need to talk to him," a woman demanded.

"What was he talking about when he said he slept with men and women?" another asked.

"And what does he mean he's not gay?"

The questions kept coming and I knew the organizer was overwhelmed. I could hardly hear his voice over the ruckus of the women, but I was going to leave all of that to him. There was no way I was going to open the door, but if I had to guess, I'd bet there were more than fifty women out there trying to get to me.

Then the organizer shouted, "I'm going to call security!"

The shouting and screaming continued and I backed away from the door. Plopping down on the sofa, I held my head in my hands.

What had I done?

My life had changed so much since I'd decided to tell my story. First, I'd been fired from the Urban League. It was really a sordid story where I'd told one of my clients that I'd let him get over if he slept with me. Little did I know it was a set-up. Little did I know that he'd recorded our whole conversation and then let his mom hear the tape.

Sam Gresham, the man who'd hired me, called me into his office to let me know that I no longer had a job. There was no way the Urban League could keep me on after that.

But while that had been a humiliating experience, in some ways, that was a blessing in disguise. I finally began to realize the consequences of my behavior, and it allowed me to take the first steps toward telling my story.

To take care of my expenses during this time, I found a part time job, working for Victoria's Secret in their call center. My focus was on telling my story—marketing myself as an HIV awareness and prevention speaker. My story was all about the DL and I was certainly an expert on that. But I was unknown, so for months, no one would book me.

Then, I received a call from someone I'd been trying to reach. The Director of HIV for the State of Ohio said that she was interested in my story and believed that other people needed to hear it, too.

"I'll make some calls for you," she said.

True to her word, she did that and within days, I received a call from Phil Wilson, the executive director of the DC AIDS Institute and that's how I'd ended up here—telling my story. But my first presentation appeared to be such a disaster...I wondered if I'd ever be asked to speak anywhere again.

Then, suddenly the door opened and the coordinator stepped inside with a woman.

"Mr. King, this is Linda Villarosa."

The young sister held out her hand for me to shake. She said, "I'm with Essence and The New York Times."

"Nice to meet you," I said, wondering why she'd been allowed to come into the room. Very quickly, she answered my question.

"I was attending this conference to do a story about a new HIV drug, but after watching you and seeing how your presentation impacted the room, I want to do a story about you for the Times. I'd like to schedule an interview, if that's okay with you."

Of course it was okay. I was being asked for an interview by the premiere newspaper in the country. I definitely wanted to speak to the New York Times.

"Okay, let's get together this afternoon," Linda said once I agreed.

We arranged for her to meet me back at my hotel, but even though she stepped out of the room, I stayed behind. The conference coordinator came back once again and asked if I'd speak to at least a few of the women who'd been in the audience.

"I'm not going to let anyone crazy come back here," he said. "But there are a few women whom I know have a few questions." When I paused, he added, "And, I did promise a Q&A after your presentation, which obviously...."

He left the rest of his sentence unspoken. Though they were paying me, I hadn't had an opportunity to finish my presentation nor answer any questions. I guess he was asking me to work just a little for the money they were paying me.

So, I agreed to speak to just a few of the women. He escorted four women inside and after the introductions, they sat down. There wasn't any small talk or any chit-chat. These women had questions and they wanted answers.

"You said you had sex with men and women. And you aren't the only man out there like that," one of the sisters said.

It was a statement, but I knew that she was really asking a question. And she was speaking for the other women. "What did you mean by that?"

So, I told them the story of the down low man, I told them my story. I told them everything—how I loved women, but slept with men. How I loved to have sex with both and I never disclosed my sexual activity to the women I was with, though most of the men knew what I was doing because they were living the same kind of life.

"I am not one in a million," I said to them. "There are so many men who have the same attitude. We have sex with each other, but we're not gay." And then, I got raw with them. "We are just men who love pussy and boy ass, but we're not gay," I repeated.

Their expressions were all the same, eyes wide, mouths open. They were in shock. Then, they started shaking their heads at the same time.

"But what about all the diseases out there, especially HIV?" one of the women asked me, almost sounding like she wanted to cry.

I shrugged. "That's one of the reasons I wanted to come here and talk to you. Because the HIV prevention message is not reaching men like me. Those messages are going to gay men. Everyone thinks gay men are the ones who are spreading HIV to each other; we think this is only their problem. But I started getting concerned when I saw the statistics—black women are the leading group of new cases, and I began to wonder if that was because of DL men."

Before, their expressions had been full of shock, but now, there was a combination of sadness and fear. And I wondered how many of them had had a casual relationship or slept with their boyfriends or even husbands without protection.

It wasn't like I was an expert on this; really, I didn't know what I was talking about. I was just spewing out facts that I'd read and assumed were true. Hell, it wasn't like I was being careful. I was fucking raw—both men and women. I didn't know my status, since I had only checked once. And like I kept telling everybody, there were so many men, especially married men who were just like me.

I answered everything that I could for the women, though I had a feeling that they still had as many questions as they'd had when they walked into that room. But it was a truth that I wanted them to know, something I believed that everyone should know.

I left the convention hall, returned to my hotel and met with Linda. She asked me all kinds of questions, many that were the same as what the women at the convention center asked me. No one could believe what I'd said—that there were men, sleeping with men, who also slept with women. I told Linda everything I knew, emphasizing the married men who were living this life. I told her about the men whose behavior was so reckless because they never used protection and exposed themselves and their wives and girlfriends to HIV. And then I told her about the men I knew who'd died from AIDs, leaving behind HIV or AIDS-infected partners.

When that article hit the front page of the New York Times, my phone started ringing off the hook. Everyone wanted to interview me, from ABC to CBS to FOX. There wasn't a major network or newspaper who didn't want to talk to J. Louis King. . . the Down Low brother.

And I was not ready. I didn't have a staff nor a publicist nor an agent to handle any of the press that was coming my way. It was just me. But that didn't bother me; I had dollar signs in my eyes. There was money to be made.

I was on a roll, taking on speaking requests and media interviews from everybody. I went from earning $500 to earning crazy money, all to talk about how DL men with their risky, selfish behavior were infecting sisters with HIV. In my talks, I now included the signs that women should look for, the ways a woman could tell if her man was sucking dick while she was working hard on her job. I kept my talks raw and real. Women needed to know the truth.

And women were appreciative...and freaking out. They were scared, but taking action, checking out their men and having conversations with their girlfriends. Everyone was talking about what J. Louis King said on BET, or what J. Louis King said in a newspaper, or where J. Louis King was speaking next and how they were definitely going to see me. Sisters wanted to meet me. They wanted to hear the answers to their questions with their own ears.

The word on the street was that J. Louis King was a sexy, good-looking bald headed brother who was a Christian, a father, said he loved dick and pussy and was not gay. I was a hot item, and not just nationally.

Then one afternoon, I got the call! From a producer on *20/20*. It seemed that Barbara Walters herself wanted to meet me. The producers told me that they would make all of my reservations and arrangements to come to New York City.

I was so excited and a few days later, made that trip to meet the producers before I would get an audience with Ms. Walters. At LaGuardia Airport, I was picked up by a limo and taken to my hotel in midtown Manhattan.

Just walking into one of the city's grand hotels made me feel like I had made it. But then it got even better when, as I was checking in, a woman walked up to me.

"Mr. King?"

"Yes." I turned to her with a smile, assuming she was part of the *20/20* team.

But then, she introduced herself. "My name is Beth Wallace, and I hope you don't mind, but I found out that you were coming to New York and I made it my business to find you. I'm a literary agent."

She talked quickly, just like a New Yorker and in less than a minute, explained that she wanted to represent me for a book deal.

"I'm not planning on writing a book," I said. I definitely didn't have any interest in that. I didn't have any problem getting on a stage and speaking, but writing? Remember, I'd barely made it out of high school! Not only did I not want to do it, I didn't think that I could.

"Are you kidding me?" she said. "You're the hottest thing in America, everyone is talking about you and your message. You know what happened with E. Lynn Harris and I can do the same thing for you. I know that I can get you at least one million dollars as an advance."

One million dollars? That was all she needed to say. I'd learn how to write; I'd figure it out. We shook hands right there, I ran up to my hotel room to drop off my bags and freshen up a bit, and then, Beth accompanied me to the lunch at Trump Towers where I was meeting the *20/20* team.

At the lunch, the producers talked to me about who I was and told me their plans for following me around for six months.

"You're going to make good TV," one of the senior producers, a sister from Boston, told me. "You have the looks, the personality that people will love."

Their plans included me moving to New York so that they could set up a life for me. They wanted to make sure that I hung out at the hottest clubs, ate at the top restaurants. They wanted to show me pulling men as well as women...and how I picked up straight men, too. It was going to be a big production.

This news, along with the million dollar deal my new agent told me about, had me up above Cloud Nine. I couldn't have been more excited. And my new agent was happy, too. She told me that a new author could not buy this kind of exposure.

"Once I get this book deal, this is going to be a best seller," she said.

I believed her. Between my new literary agent and *20/20*, I left New York City feeling like I had arrived.

But then, my plane landed back in Ohio. And although I'd just been kissed by the mighty *20/20* producers, I felt sad... because I didn't have anyone to share this news with. I wanted to call up everyone I knew, tell all of my family and friends. But to be honest, I couldn't because I carried such a spirit of shame with the life I'd led. The truth was, I wasn't happy with myself and my behavior then, or now.

So I kept all the good news inside. I didn't say a single word to anyone. All I did was silently celebrate with me, myself and I.

CHAPTER 16

I Am An Author...Or Not...

*g*etting a book deal was not as easy as the agent told me it would be. In fact, just a month after that meeting with the *20/20* team, Beth dropped me because she didn't understand the DL message. She just didn't get it.

And, she called me up to tell me. "I'm sorry, Mr. King, but I'm going to have to let you go. I don't think I'll be able to get a book deal."

"Why not?"

"Because people are looking for the next E. Lynn Harris and while your book might be interesting, it doesn't have the broad appeal that his books have."

Not broad enough? Was she kidding? If I were to write this book, not only would every African American woman *want* to read it, but she would *need* to read it. I tried to tell Beth that, but she would not be moved.

"Well, whatever, I don't think I can sell it, but I wish you the best of luck."

I'm sure she probably wanted to jump off the Brooklyn bridge once my book made the New York Times Bestseller's List, but at the time that she made that call to me, I didn't know what the future was going to bring. All I knew was that when I hung up the phone from her, I was devastated. Not only had Beth put the idea of writing a book into my head, but she'd left me with that dream of a million dollars.

What was I supposed to do now? How was I supposed to make that happen? I didn't know where to go; it wasn't like I knew anyone in the publishing industry. That telephone call felt like rejection and left me dejected. My dreams were over even before they had a chance to begin.

But then, I remembered the vision I'd had—how God had told me that He wanted me to tell my story. And how He'd be with me...all I had to do was trust Him.

So, I took my concerns to God. I prayed and asked Him to show me what to do now. Then, I became still. I had no other choice but to wait and see how God would work this out.

And of course, He did. One day, I got a call from a gentleman named Manie Barron.

"I heard that you needed new representation," he said after he told me that he was an agent with William Morris. "I would love to represent you."

I had never heard of Manie Barron, so I asked if I could call him back the next day. He agreed and I used that time to do a little research. It didn't take much for me to find out that he was one of the top African Americans in the literary community, first working his way up at Random House and now considered a top agent, especially since he was with the well-respected and highly acclaimed William Morris agency.

So first thing the next day, I called him back and told him yes—that I would love for him to represent me.

"Great," Manie said. "The first thing we're going to need is an inquiry package."

"What's that?"

"It's a package that we'll send out to the publishers to tell them all about you, tell them about what you've done, what makes you an expert in this field. Essentially, we're going to tell your story and why it needs to be published."

That sounded logical to me. "Okay," I said. "Let's do this."

"I can do an inquiry package for you for twenty thousand dollars," Manie said so casually you would've thought he was talking about the weather.

Twenty thousand dollars?

WTF...was what I wanted to say to him. I didn't have twenty dollars let alone $20,000.

My silence let Manie know that I was in shock. "I know that sounds like a lot of money," he said, "but it's really necessary if you want to get the type of deal your story deserves."

He went on to explain the process, how publishers really pay attention to inquiry packages, especially when a book has yet to be written. "And you're new," he said. "This package will get people to know you."

By the time he finished, I knew that I had to do it. I was hungry for this to happen, and I wanted the process to move forward. I didn't have any choice; I hired Manie to get this done.

I borrowed the five thousand dollars that Manie said he needed to get started from my dad, and then, I sat back and waited. About a week later, I received Manie's inquiry package—it was a three-page letter and inside was also a bill for $15,000.

Once again, Manie had left me in shock, but then he took it up a level—he dropped me. Yes, I was dropped again.

His excuse? "I'm just too busy right now; I won't be able to give you the attention that this project will need."

Again, I was devastated—but at least I wouldn't have to pay him the remaining fifteen thousand dollars. This time, though, my disappointment didn't last long. Manie referred me to another agent with William Morris.

"I'm sure he'll be excited to work with you," Manie said.

So, in came Ian Klienart. After a short conversation, he signed me and sent that inquiry package out. He put the book up for auction and within forty-eight hours, received multiple bids from some of the largest publishers. They all wanted to bid on this book.

I was ecstatic, but Ian was a pro. "The deal is not done yet," he said.

Ian set a deadline and started a bidding war among the publishers. By the time the auction ended, Random House offered the most money and the sweetest deal. It was done!

I cannot tell you how thrilled I was. Not only to finally have a book deal, but Random House was where my personal role model and super New York Times best selling author, Mr. E. Lynn Harris was published. In fact, Janet Hill, who was Lynn's editor, was the editor who won the bid. E. Lynn had told her to get my book and she did.

Once all the contracts were executed, I was assigned to Karen Hunter to co-author the book with me.

Karen Hunter, a Pulitzer Prize-winning journalist and author was a celebrity ghost writer. From LL Cool J to Wendy Williams and Al Sharpton, Karen had penned many best-selling celebrity books.

To me, that was a sign that Random House believed in me. They'd brought out the big guns to work on my book...and I was ready. I couldn't wait to get started.

CHAPTER 17

New Beginnings

*I*t seemed that just about every part of my life was changing. Not only did I finally have a book deal, but I moved from Columbus to Chicago...to be with a man. I'd met this brother at a sex party in Chicago during a quick trip I'd taken there one weekend. This party was a small private event, but that's how I met Peter. Naked. At a party.

He was tall, handsome, charming and naked. Out of all the men there, I was taken with him right away. For the next few months we saw each other often; he'd come to Columbus to see me or I'd fly to Chicago to see him. Our connection was instant, and it wasn't long before I was in love. And Peter was in love with me. So much so, that he asked me to leave Columbus and move to Chicago with him.

Peter didn't have to ask me twice. Chicago! The big city! The Windy City! The city of tall buildings and that lake! *Hell, yeah!* I was moving to Chicago!

Moving with Peter just seemed to be that icing on the cake that was my life at the time. Everything was working: I had my book deal, I had received a nice check, a very hefty check as part of my advance, I was speaking around the country, *20/20* was still working on their segment about my life...moving to a big city seemed perfect.

"And, I want you to come so that you can really concentrate on writing," Peter told me. "If we're living together, you won't have to worry about anything. I really believe in you and this book and I want to help make this happen for you."

He kept his promise. Peter provided me with an amazing home, and a great life. Like most of the people in my life whom I'd dated to that point, Peter took care of me. He cooked, he cleaned, he did everything that I needed. I was able to focus on the book full-time.

Peter also provided me with a link that I was missing—family. I didn't spend much time with mine, always using the excuse that Springfield was so far away. But Peter's grandmother, Sarah Peterson, lived in Indiana, not too far from the Illinois border. On Sundays, we'd go to worship with her in her small Baptist church, and then afterward, we go to her home for dinner—one of those Soul Food Sunday dinners that black grandmothers and mothers are so famous for.

I would sit around with Peter's family—his cousins, aunts and uncles—for hours, feeling at home, feeling accepted, completely accepted as Peter's partner.

At our home, Peter gave me all the space I needed to do what I had to do. In fact, I spent most weekends in New York, working with Karen Hunter in a hotel suite in Manhattan. Karen was no joke; she knew what she was doing. She knew how to tell a story.

"I just want the truth," she said to me. "No fluff, no lies, no drama...just the truth. Because if your book reads like a lie, you'll pay for it for the rest of your life."

So, I told Karen the truth and we went to work. And then every Monday, I returned to Chicago and to Peter.

Even though we'd been together for almost a year, it still felt like a new relationship since I'd only been in Chicago for a few months and I was traveling all the time. So whenever we were together, it was fresh. We enjoyed doing all kinds of things together, especially taking walks through the neighborhood. That was one thing that I really loved to do—walking and taking in the sights of Chicago, especially the beautiful homes on the North side.

One afternoon as we were walking and talking, and I noticed this fat, light-skinned brother speed-walking toward us. Peter had been talking and then, he suddenly stopped... stopped talking and walking.

This guy walked up to us and swung on Peter so hard, he knocked him to the ground. Right there on the street. Then, he started kicking him and cursing, calling him all kinds of 'bitches' and 'motherfuckers'.

"Your bitch ass belongs to me!" he screamed.

I was standing there, dumbfounded and in shock when he turned to me. "Who the fuck are you?" he asked. Before I could say a word, he continued, "Don't you know this is my bitch? I own his ass and I will kill him!"

This guy was beyond pissed and I was beyond scared.

I didn't say a word, but I guess he didn't expect me to because he turned right back to Peter. "Get your ass up and go home. I'm coming over!"

He looked at me again. "And your ass better not be there when I get there, or I'm going to knock your ass out, too, bitch ass nigga!"

Then, he walked off, just as suddenly as he came.

It still took a moment for it to all register, but when I looked down at Peter, it really hit me. Peter looked like he'd been beaten badly; his nose was bleeding, one eye was swollen and he was still trembling.

My eyes were wide as I looked at him.

"I'm so sorry," he cried. I guess he was apologizing for the fear he saw written all over my face.

"Who the hell was that? What's going on?" I yelled. I wasn't the most sympathetic man at that moment; I didn't care that he was beaten and bleeding. I just wanted him to explain what had just happened.

Here I was in Chicago, had just moved here to be with Peter, and now, I was being told by some crazy-ass man that I'd better not be in the home where I'd been living? I was scared as hell and had no place to go.

"I'm sorry," Peter repeated.

I repeated my questions to him. He needed to give me some kind of explanation.

"That was DJ," he said as if I was supposed to know who DJ was. "We have to get back to my place and you have to pack!" he said, shaking even more.

"I have to pack?"

He nodded. "Yeah, you can't be there when he gets there. Didn't you hear what he said?"

I was fuming as we rushed back to what I thought was our home. I didn't say a word to Peter as I packed and called hotels at the same time. I needed to find some place that wasn't too expensive. And some place where I could check in now!

As I gathered together all of my shit, I just couldn't believe this was happening to me. I had five suitcases, my computer, and the printed manuscript of my book that I was still working on. Even though I had all of that stuff, it didn't take me long to get it together. I saw what DJ had done to Peter; I wasn't going to wait to see what he would do to me. And Peter helped to get me out of there, too—a cab was waiting when I came downstairs with all of my things.

"I'll call you later," Peter told me as he helped me load everything that I'd brought to Chicago into the taxi.

Thank God I was able to find a reasonably priced room at the Sheraton on Michigan Avenue. But that was the only thing that I felt good about; I was still scared and so confused.

Within an hour, though, I began to calm down. I checked into my hotel room that had a beautiful (soothing) view of Lake Michigan. I got settled in, ordered up two drinks, took a shower, then laid across the massive bed. Even though I was calmer, I couldn't get the image of that big, yella Negro out of my mind. I saw him again and again, knocking Peter down. Screaming at Peter, telling me that Peter was his. Peter, the man that I'd loved, that I'd uprooted my life for. Peter, the man who I had planned to build a life with. Peter, who was my partner on this journey of becoming an author.

But I wasn't about to put my life at risk for any man, or any woman for that matter. So after about a week, I moved into an apartment and while I was crazy enough to continue to see Peter on the side, I also started meeting other brothers in Chicago.

I especially loved getting together with men who weren't into the gay lifestyle. Men who hosted private house parties and didn't let their business get out. It was a new kind of freedom for me. I'd been single for many years, but now, I was single in this beautiful big city.

It was a blissful few months. Flying between New York and Chicago working on my book, meeting lots of professional men, and then, I was seeing the man that I loved on the side.

Peter and I began to see each other more and more—especially once I found out that DJ was married!

Yes! The fat dude who had kicked Peter's ass had a wife at home who made sure that DJ didn't have too much freedom himself. That's why I was able to live with Peter for as long as I did before DJ showed up. Between me still being in Peter's life and his wife at home, I guess DJ finally saw that there wasn't much of a chance for him to have any kind of real life with Peter.

So once DJ went away, I gave up the Chicago single life and moved back in with Peter. But I didn't want to stay in the same place where he'd been with DJ. I was never really sure that DJ wouldn't show up again. I wanted to move far away from that place.

Peter and I set up house in a townhome on the West side of Chicago in an area called Millionaire's Row. It was two blocks of full-of-character, older homes that had once been occupied by only millionaires. We settled in, even got a dog named Mae, and began our life together. We became one of the 'it' couples in Chicago, who worked hard during the week, entertained friends when I was in town over the weekends, and traveled whenever we could.

Life with Peter, life in Chicago, life as an up and coming author was very, very good.

CHAPTER 18

Nothing but the Truth

*T*here were many days when I would ask myself, how in the hell did I get here? I was still working on the manuscript, still speaking, and I had the most anticipated book in America. My only job was to continue to write, to keep speaking, and to keep folks talking about me.

It was such a good time professionally, but personally as well, though not in the way you would think. You would think that with the way Peter was taking care of me, spoiling me, that I would've been totally happy at home. And in a way, I was.

Peter took care of me, he put me on his company's health insurance, he provided financial support when I needed it; he continued to spoil me in every way. But while he went to work every day, I cheated on him non-stop.

He would leave home at eight in the morning, and by nine, I had some other dude up in our place. I was home all day, so I had lots of time to play around and sample some of the finest men in Chicago. I just couldn't stop cheating on the people who loved me; I couldn't stop being deceptive in my relationships.

At the time, I didn't question it, but years later, I did. Why did I do this to the people I loved? After seeking the answer to that question, I found out that I had a sexual addiction. All I wanted was sex sex sex sex sex and more sex sex sex.

I know many, especially women, don't believe in sexual addiction. I've heard women say that this was just some fake disease invented by men as an excuse for their deviant behavior. But sexual addiction is a mental health disorder affliction recognized by most in the medical community, including the American Psychiatric Association. I can tell you there were times in my life when I really wanted to stop and just couldn't. There were times when I hated myself for what I was doing to other people, but I couldn't find a way to change my behavior.

At this time though, I didn't see any reason to change. I felt as if the world was talking about me—in a good way. Everyone was telling me that they couldn't wait for my book, that I was going to be so big, that I was going to change the world. Hearing that every day, it's no wonder that I let that go to my head. My ego swelled up and it would've stayed there if Random House didn't bring me down a few notches.

It happened during the first editorial reading of *On the Down Low*. Karen and I had finished the three-hundred page manuscript. We'd worked hard and I'd accumulated lots of frequent flyer miles in the process. I was looking forward to hearing all the accolades from the folks at Random House.

When I arrived at the Random House offices, I was led to a conference room overlooking Times Square. The room was filled with editors and the heads of most of the departments.

Janet Hill sat at the head of the table and smiled as I entered. I greeted everyone, and then noticed my manuscript in front of Janet. Now, I was really excited. I just knew Janet was going to tell me that this was one of the best books she'd ever read and that we were going to sell millions upon millions of copies.

When I sat down at the table, Janet spoke first. "Mr. King, if you're not willing to give the readers the truth about yourself, then I don't want to publish this book, and you can just refund the advance you received."

I was shocked. *Really?* Those were the first words that she had for me? This had to be some kind of joke.

But Janet was very serious. She continued, "The story you told me when we first signed you and the story that's in this book are two different stories. And I want the truth. Your book is important and will definitely be one of the most talked about books in the country, but I will only proceed if this is right, if this is the truth. We want the real story." She tapped the manuscript in front of her and added, "And this right here is not the true story."

I sat there not knowing what to say, even though millions of thoughts were going through my mind. My feelings were hurt by that meeting (the other editors and executives all said the same thing) but, I had to go home and regroup. I had to pray and ask God to give me the strength to tell it all. I had to ask Him to guide me to do what He told me to do.

I'd left out lots of things in the book—so many secrets. But the thing was, even though many of the situations that I'd kept out of the book would help people, it would put all of my business right out there on front street. Everything would be there in the public eye.

But after a few days of really thinking about it and really praying, I knew that not only was Janet completely right, but I had to do what she told me to do. I had come too far to turn around. I had to tell the truth.

So, I returned to New York and that hotel suite and I told Karen what I didn't want to tell her before. I told her how I'd been fired from too many positions for propositioning men. I told her about how I'd been sexing ministers. I told her that I'd had sex with so many married men, always without protection. And I told her about my own AIDs scare. I told her everything.

It was hard to reveal so many secrets about my life. And not just because of me, but because I knew there were things I had to say that would hurt other people, things that would destroy my family and make me an outcast.

The thing was, telling Karen the truth would show people who thought they knew little Jimmy King, that they really didn't know me at all. Everyone was going to find out that I wasn't the pure and straight son of Deacon Louis and Lillie Mae. (Although much of that image had been shot when Brenda and I divorced.) But folks would read about the dark side of me, things I'd done to my friends, past girlfriends, my military buddies and my extended family.

And then there was my church family. My father still attended the same church and everyone there would know that Jimmy King was really JL King, the brother on the down low. And that one little incident that happened with Melvin... well, it wasn't so little after all. It hadn't been a mistake, and sleeping with men had become my life.

The smart thing I could've done at that point was get in touch with some people, especially my friends and family. But I didn't and that was a cowardly move that I regret to this day. I wish that I'd been man enough to call the people closest to me to tell them that I was writing a book about who I really was. I wished that I hadn't let everyone that I loved get blind-sided with a book they never expected and a life that they never suspected. (Remember, I was good at hiding who I was; I'd been good at it for years. And after Brenda and I divorced, my family only saw me with women.)

But I didn't do what I was supposed to do and when my book finally came out with the truth that Random House wanted, my friends and family were hit hard. After that, many of the people from my past didn't want to have anything to do with me and the cost of losing them, especially my extended family, has been very painful.

That was just one of the millions of things in my life that I wish that I could do over. That was one of the greatest mistakes I'd ever made.

Another one of the do-overs that I wish that I could do was with Peter. Even with having to go back and revise my manuscript, my life was still moving fast. Random House was still behind me, I was still getting lots of requests, and all of that put a strain on my relationship with Peter. He started to get a little bit jealous. And then, it got worse and worse and worse....

CHAPTER 19

Reality Check

*I*t took us a couple of months, but Karen and I finally finished the manuscript and this time, Janet Hill approved it and we were able to turn it over for the final edits.

I left New York City feeling particularly good as I headed back to Chicago. I expected that my book would hit the shelves in a couple of months. Especially since Janet asked me not to do any more media.

"We don't want you overexposed before the book is released," she told me. "That will hurt sales. So any requests you get, turn them over to your in-house publicist."

That was fine with me, except that every interview request I sent over to my publicist, she turned down. It was frustrating. Not only did I want to keep doing media so that my name would stay out there, but this was how I made most of my money—through speaking engagements.

After a couple of months, I stopped sending the requests to Random House and I started doing the interviews without their permission. I didn't think I would have to take on too many because my book would be coming out very soon. But then, the weeks kept going by. And the weeks turned into months. Finally, all those months turned into a year and I still hadn't heard a word from Random House. We'd turned that book in at the beginning of 2002, and now, here we were at the beginning of 2003, and I knew nothing more.

When in the hell was my book going to be released? I kept wondering. What was going on? It wasn't like I was sitting back waiting. Every week I called Janet to get an update, but I could never get her on the phone.

Then in mid 2003, I got a call.

"Mr. King, when can you come to New York?" one of the publicity assistants asked me. "We have to do a photo shoot for the book cover."

Finally, we were making progress. Once again, I was excited, and this time, I asked Peter to go with me. We'd been having problems; it seemed like we were always arguing, and arguing about nothing. I suspected that it was because of all the attention I was getting. So, I wanted to include Peter and I thought this trip would do us both good.

We flew to New York (on their dime), and after Peter and I checked into the hotel, we went to Random House for a meeting with my publicist. She gave me a five thousand dollar credit card for Saks Fifth Avenue so that I could shop for the shoot, and right after the meeting, Peter and I headed to the store. I went straight to the exclusive designer floor, and spent the five thousand dollars on three outfits.

The shoot, the next day was one of the most amazing experiences of my life to that point. I was treated like royalty as Random House took me to a warehouse on the West side. There were about twenty people there to pamper me—to do everything from shave me, dress me, and make sure that my skin was flawless for the camera. We did a number of different poses, and it took hours. Even though it was exciting, as the day went by, I became exhausted. When the photographer finally said that it was a wrap, I was grateful.

The only negative part was that while I was being treated grandly by Random House, Peter was giving me drama. The trip had started out fine, but by the time we were on set for the shoot, he started acting a fool!

As he watched me at the shoot, I could see his mood become darker and darker. I tried to include him to prevent a blow-up. I asked him how did I look, and which outfit he preferred. But everything turned into an argument. The man who had been my rock had turned into the biggest pain in the ass. He was stealing the joy of this journey, making me pray all through the shoot. I was so stressed out that I wasn't sure how the pictures were going to turn out even though the photographer had told me that I'd done well.

Peter didn't lighten up until the next day when we returned to Chicago. My expectation was that my book was going to be fast-tracked now. Within weeks, a month, the latest, I expected that I'd be given a release date.

But just like before, the weeks turned into months and I still hadn't heard a thing. What I didn't know at the time, but would later find out was that much of the delay had to do with Random House seriously considering pulling the book and not releasing it at all.

I learned from a source (that to this day, I cannot name), that the president of Random House had received telephone calls from several influential black men asking that my book not be published. He was told that my book would do great harm to the black community and to black men specifically.

The president actually called together his executive staff to discuss the situation as he felt the pressure mounting. But after lots of back and forth, lots of long meetings and discussions, it was decided that Random House would proceed.

It seems that even before the book was born, folks were scared of the truth and I knew why. My book would be hitting too close to home for the many movers and shakers in the entertainment industry, in politics, in sports. And then there was the biggest group against me—the faith-based leaders who I understand were ready to fight me in every way possible to stop this story from coming out.

A few years later after my book came out, I read in the New York Post that the president of Random House had said that releasing my book was the smartest business decision he made in 2004. He said that *On the Down Low* was one of the top sellers that year and he was glad that his company had published it.

And I know he was glad because without even knowing it, Random House was about to get the best publicity they could ever get for my book.

CHAPTER 20

Oprah? Oprah? Is that you?

*T*he one situation that was truly going to change my life went down like this: I was in the kitchen, fixing breakfast for me and Peter. It was one of those crisp, clear, beautiful Chicago days. A normal day...or so I thought.

The phone rang and after I said hello, the caller asked, "Is this JL?"

I didn't recognize the voice. So I said, "Yeah, who dis," in my best urban impression.

"Mr. King, this is Terri. I'm a producer with HARPO and the Oprah Winfrey show. How are you?"

Yeah, right!

I pressed the phone closer to my ear, trying to figure out which one of my friends thought this prank was funny. "Who dis?"

She repeated what she'd just told me. "Terri Mitchell. I'm a producer with HARPO and Oprah would like to talk to you about your new book and being a guest on her show. Are you interested?"

I was just not in the mood for whoever was playing this joke, so I just hung up. It was a ridiculous prank anyway. As if Oprah would really call and say she wanted to talk about my book. A book that hadn't even come out yet. She wanted me to come on the most powerful show to talk to the most powerful woman.

Yeah, right!

Whoever that was on the other end of the phone had just gotten the dial tone.

Then, my cell rang again. It was a different number than before, but still not a number that I recognized—well, except for the 312 area code.

After I said hello, I heard. "JL, this is Terri Mitchell from HARPO. We must have been disconnected. But anyway, I'd like to meet with you. Are you available to come to the studio this week?"

Okay, so someone had serious jokes. They were going to play this all the way through, so I decided to play, too. "Sure, I'll come and meet with Oprah and discuss my new book." It took everything that I had not to bust out laughing.

"Okay," this Terri person said. "I'll have one of our associate producers follow up with you for a time. Have a great day." And this time, *she* hung up.

I stared at the phone for a second.

Yeah, right!

Since I couldn't figure out who was playing this joke on me, I pushed it out of my head. Until Peter came down and asked, "Who was on the phone, baby?"

And with a straight face, I said, "Wrong number. Let's eat."

Even though I knew the call was a joke, I still didn't want Peter to know about it. Things hadn't gotten any better between us. He was still watching my every move and my spirit was telling me to stop sharing my blessings with him. Not that I thought that call was a blessing. I knew it wasn't Oprah, but I made it a policy to share very little with Peter. I had to, if I wanted to keep the peace and keep my sanity, too.

CHAPTER 21

The Big Time!

I couldn't believe it. I was actually going to be on *The Oprah Winfrey Show*!

It turned out that call that I'd received two weeks before was the real deal. But I didn't realize it until Terri called to actually schedule my interview.

"Wait, who is this?" I asked when Terri called again.

She repeated what she'd told me before, that she was a producer on *The Oprah Winfrey Show* and that Oprah wanted to do a show about HIV and black women and she wanted me as one of her guests. It seemed that not only had Oprah read an advance copy of the book, but she'd heard about my speeches and seminars.

This time I believed Terri, and after I picked myself up from the floor, I had a great conversation with her about DL men and HIV in the black community.

"This is going to be a great show for our viewers," Terri told me. "Oprah's going to have several people on, but you'll be one of the ones that she'll talk to from home base."

"Home base?"

Terri went on to explain that home base was the two leather couches where Oprah interviewed her guests. "You'll probably be the third segment of the show, from commercial to commercial."

It was hard to contain my excitement and you know my publisher was so excited as well. My book had still not been officially scheduled for release but with the call from Oprah, you know all of that changed, right? Suddenly, I had a release date—not in time for Oprah, but people would be able to do preorders.

So not only was I going to be on *Oprah*, but finally, my book was going to be on the shelves. The only thing was that once I was scheduled for *Oprah*, *20/20* went out the window. I had no idea how they found out; not that I cared when they called to cancel. It had been more than two years—they were moving as slow as Random House. Oprah wanted me now!

After I had all of my business handled with my editor and everyone at Random House, I called my daughter, Ebony.

When I told her that I was going on *Oprah*, she said, "Oh, my God! I want to go!"

"You got it, baby girl."

I arranged for Ebony to join me and the Oprah team reserved two rooms for us at the Omni Hotel, where all of the HARPO guests stayed.

The night before the show, I packed my bag to head over to the hotel. Ebony had flown in earlier and we were going to have dinner. Of course, I couldn't wait to see my daughter and catch up with what had been going on in her life. But I wanted to get together with Ebony for another reason—I wanted to tell her what I was going to say on the show. I had never discussed my sexual orientation with my children. And although many in Springfield, Ohio knew what had happened, my children had been sheltered from the true reason for their parents divorcing. Plus, they'd only seen me with women, never a man. I wasn't sure what they knew. So, I wanted to tell Ebony what I was going to say. I wanted her to be prepared.

Just as I zipped up my bag, Peter came stomping into the room. "Where are you going?" he asked.

As soon as he said that, I knew he was trippin'. Against my better judgment, I'd told Peter about Oprah calling. After all, that would've been a hard secret to keep anyway. Up to this point, Peter had been cool, just a little sullen.

The way he looked at me now, though, let me know that was about to change.

"You know where I'm going," I said as I lifted the bag off the bed.

"Well, you don't need to go. I'm not gonna support any of this stuff anymore. Not the book, not the show; you don't need to do any of it."

Was he kidding me? Then, he did something he'd never done before—Peter started crying. And, I'm not talking about tears just rolling down his face. I'm talking about boo-hoo kind of crying. He was weeping like someone died.

"I don't want you to leave me," he shouted. "Don't go to the hotel."

"I have to," I said. "You know Ebony is waiting for me."

"Just let her stay there. She's a big girl, she can handle it. But you can't leave me."

"You just want me to leave her at the hotel by herself?" I asked. I was hoping that if I repeated what he told me, it would sound as ridiculous to him as it sounded to me.

But I guess it didn't because he just said, "Yes, leave her there."

The way he was crying and shaking, I knew Peter had to be having some kind of mental breakdown.

"You don't care anything about us! You're just off living your life, not caring about me or anything! After everything that I've done for you!"

I stood there looking at him, thinking that this was supposed to be one of the best times of my life. I was about to go on Oprah's show to discuss my new book and I had to deal with this? Like he'd done many times before, Peter was killing my joy. The most exciting time of my life and he was trippin'.

My plan had been to ask Peter to drop me off at the hotel, but I decided that he didn't need to have anything to do with this. I called a cab and as I waited, I had to listen to him rant and rave about nothing.

Thankfully, the cab came pretty quickly. Peter was still screaming when I jumped into the cab, but then do you know what that fool did? Right when we pulled away from our home he jumped into his car and followed us. I kept looking through the back window, not believing what I was seeing. He followed the cab all the way to the Omni.

He had taken crazy to a whole 'nother level. When I got out of the cab, he illegally parked behind us, leapt out of his car and accosted me as I stepped into the lobby.

"I thought I told you not to go," he said.

"Peter," I said, looking around at the hotel guests who were staring at us without shame. I guess I had enough shame for everyone. I was so embarrassed as Peter grabbed my arm, trying to stop me from walking to the front desk and the whole time he was shouting and crying.

When hotel security approached us and asked if everything was okay, I told them that I was a guest at the hotel, but Peter was not and that he needed to leave. He was still screaming and crying when the police escorted him out.

The last words I heard before he walked out the hotel's doors were, "Don't leave me! I know you're going to leave me after you go on *Oprah*!"

Peter and I had not discussed breaking up, though I guess he knew what I knew...we were headed that way. And I guess somewhere inside of him, he also knew that leaving him right after the *Oprah* show was definitely my plan.

As I stood at the front desk, I was just grateful that Ebony hadn't been downstairs to witness that scene. I don't know how I did it, but I got myself together, checked into my room and then called my daughter to meet me in the hotel's restaurant. Ebony, my baby girl, my firstborn was still (and would always be) the apple of my eye. But now, I had to face her and tell her the truth of my life.

I didn't wait long to tell her the news. After we hugged and placed our orders, I got right to my point. "So, I wanted to tell you what I'll be talking about tomorrow on Oprah."

"I'm so excited," Ebony said. "And, I'm so proud of you."

In that moment, I realized for the first time how nervous I was about this talk. My ex-wife and I had kept the truth about our break-up from our children to protect them, but now I wondered, how much of that was all about me? Had I just been trying to protect myself?

"So, what are you going to be talking about?" my daughter asked me.

Taking a deep breath, I said, "I'm going to be speaking about men who live on the down low. Men who...have sex. With men. And with women." I paused and then added, "I'm going to be talking about my life."

I held my breath, waiting for the barrage of questions, not sure exactly how I was going to answer everything that Ebony wanted to know.

And then she said, "I love you, dad. And, I'm proud of you."

That was it! Nothing more. She just started talking about what she was going to wear to the show, school, her mom. It was as if what I said didn't matter at all.

So, I sat back and enjoyed my daughter. And together, over dinner and cocktails, we shared our excitement about being on *The Oprah Winfrey Show.*

The day of the show I still could hardly believe that I was there. Once Ebony and I were in the green room, the producers told me once again that I was going to be one of several guests who would sit with Oprah on the platform on the leather couch.

"You're going to be on the third segment of the show, JL," she told me once again.

Then, Ebony and I were escorted into the studio where the show was taped. As I sat in the front row next to my daughter, I was in awe. How many times had I seen this scene on television? And now, here I sat.

The other guests were also seated on the front row: HIV Activist Phil Wilson of the AIDS Institute in DC was the expert that day and he would be going onto the stage first. There were also women who were HIV positive because of their husbands in the audience who were told they would be sitting on home base to tell their stories. All of us would be on the stage at various times during the program.

Behind us were my guests that I'd invited: Peter (who had called me the night before begging me to forgive him), Margena Christian, the Features editor with *Jet* magazine, and Art Sims, a Chicago socialite and very close friend of mine.

And then, there was the audience—a room full of women who had no idea what this show was going to be about.

Every emotion known to man filled me. I was nervous and excited. A little bit scared and anxious. I was happy about what I was about to do, but sad that this was the first time people close to me were going to hear the story.

But one thing—I was dressed right and looking good.

Then, Oprah came out and everyone stood and applauded. I didn't think it was possible, but I was even more excited right then. I was standing in front of the Queen of Talk. Oprah didn't like meeting her guests before the show; she wanted the experience of talking to them and hearing their stories with the audience.

"Thank you everyone," she said when the audience quieted down. She waited until we all took our seats to add, "I've been asked to do shows about HIV and Black women for years and I never really thought it would be a good topic for the *Oprah* show. But recently, I read a story in the Chicago Tribune that touched me and I told my producers, it was time. So today this show is about HIV and you also will learn about a behavior called living on the down low with author JL King. I learned about this from reading JL's book. It was an amazing, riveting story that I wanted to share."

Then she took her seat on home base and every eye in the studio was on her. Especially mine. I was just feet away from Oprah...the miracle worker, the sister who turned books into best sellers. I was shivering with excitement.

There was a pause as all the cameras got into place; I guess a commercial was on. And then, one of the producers came down to me. "Oprah wants you to join her on the couch.

"Me?" I asked, pointing to my chest. "I thought I was going to be the third person on the show."

"Oprah wants you to join her right now."

I looked past him as if I was checking with Oprah because the last thing I wanted was for this dude to be mistaken and then I looked like a fool standing up. But Oprah smiled, nodded and motioned for me to come up to the stage.

Turning to my daughter, I shrugged, then stood up and headed to the interview that was truly going to change my life more than I could have possibly known.

I sat down, the producers mic'd me up, and Oprah leaned over and said to me, "Gayle and I loved your book. It was such an interesting read." Then, she patted my book that was in her lap.

"Thank you," I said.

"Okay, let's get ready to sell some books."

In that second, that vision and God's words played back for me once again. And I knew that everything that God said He would do, He was doing right now. Because sitting there with Oprah was nothing but God.

The show opened and Oprah began asking me questions about my life. I told her the truth—that I loved women and I loved men. But I wasn't gay!

"How can that be?" she asked.

She said that she'd never really heard about the down low experience before she read my book and that she and Gayle were fascinated by it. But she seemed more fascinated by the fact that I wouldn't classify myself into a category.

"So you're not gay?" she asked me more than once.

"No."

Then, there was the first commercial break and just as I was getting ready to stand, Oprah told the producers, "No, I want JL to stay up here with me."

"But what about...."

"I'll talk to them from up here," Oprah said, referring to her other guests.

From that point on, the show didn't go the way I thought it would. I sat with Oprah for the entire hour. We talked, we laughed. I told her after one of the breaks that I thought my daughter was having a hard time with this conversation.

Oprah said, "I know, I can tell. I'm going to talk to her."

So she went to Ebony and asked, "What do you think of your dad?"

Ebony said, "I love him and I'm proud of him."

Tears welled up in my eyes because although Ebony had said the exact same thing last night, I wasn't sure what she would say after she actually heard me talking about my life in front of a national audience. Oprah glanced at me, then winked as if to say, 'I got you.'

Right before the end of the show, Oprah held up my book and said, "Go buy this book. Everyone needs to read this—*On the Down Low*, by JL King."

She'd said that to millions of her viewers!

When the final credits rolled, the producers removed the microphones from me and Oprah before she asked, "Are we going to do the after show?"

"No," the guy told her. "We didn't plan to do that."

"Well, we should. I want to continue this conversation."

So they set up my mic once again, and we continued talking for another thirty minutes.

Afterward, I took a picture with Oprah and by the time I walked out of the studios, I was floating, feeling like I was on a serious high. I thought back to the vision and the words of God. He was fulfilling all of that for me that day.

But then, I left the HARPO studios in the limo with Ebony and the two other ladies and I reflected back on everything that I'd said. And regret began to seep in fast. Had I really said all of that? Had I really revealed myself to the world that way? I couldn't imagine what strangers would think of me. What about my friends and family?

I began to wonder—what would the consequences of this day be?

No matter what I imagined, I was completely unprepared for what was to come. That day changed my life. I was introduced as the Down Low Brother. And the world had a melt down.

CHAPTER 22

OMG! Did you see Oprah?

For the three weeks between when the show was taped and when it would air, my doubts continued to grow. But I tried to push all of my negative thoughts aside. Maybe it would be fine. Maybe I came off more positively than I believed.

Peter, who was acting supportive, which was so out of character for him recently, had been able to calm my fears just a bit. "You were great," he kept telling me. "In fact, I think we should host a viewing party."

"Really?"

"Yeah, let's have all of our friends over and we'll watch it together. I'll do all the planning."

For Peter to want to do that had to mean that I had nothing to fear. So I allowed Peter to sweep me away in his enthusiasm and I began to look forward to the party.

When the caterers arrived on the day of the party, I couldn't believe all that Peter had put together. That night, about a dozen of our friends and associates, both straight and gay, joined us at our condo to watch the second airing of Oprah's show. Back in the day, Oprah came on twice in Chicago—once in the morning and again, that night. We'd told our friends not to watch the first airing; we'd watch it all together.

It was a festive affair, a night full of food, drink and laughter. And then, we watched the show.

For the most part, everyone was quiet, taking it in, sharing their (positive) thoughts during the commercials. My friends said that I looked good, that what I was saying was the truth, that the show was great.

But my opinion differed from theirs. In fact, watching the show was pure hell for me. Everything that I'd been thinking was true—I hated the way I came across. I didn't like the person who was sitting on that couch next to Oprah. I was an arrogant fool, talking shit. It sounded like I didn't have a clue as to what my life and behavior was doing to others—my family and friends and the relationships that I'd been in. This was just another time in my life when I wished that I could have a do-over. There were so many important things that I needed to say, that people needed to hear. But I was sure that my demeanor had trumped my words and I was sorry about that.

I couldn't wait for the party to end, I didn't want to celebrate another minute of that show. When our final guest left, I checked my cell phone. I'd had it off most of the day, and I had dozens of messages.

Not really feeling like talking to anyone, I got on-line instead and when I logged into my email account, I couldn't believe it. I had thousands of emails—almost ten thousand to be exact. I didn't know that an email account could hold that many messages.

I logged off without reading a single one. But, I didn't move from the desk; all I could do was sit there and think about all the phone messages, all the email messages. I knew every one of them had to do with the *Oprah* show and it felt like my life had been invaded.

"Are you okay?" Peter asked, as he peeked into our second bedroom that doubled as an office.

"Yeah."

"Well you need to come to bed. This has been quite a day."

There was no need for me to go to bed. I knew I wouldn't be able to sleep. Not with the way I felt. My heart was so heavy and so I told Peter that I needed to pray.

Peter left me alone, but I wasn't just saying that to get rid of him. I really did need to pray. I needed to talk to God about this and get His guidance once again. This was His doing, so I really needed to know where to go from here. There was no way I was going to be able to do this without Him.

So, I got on my knees.

Our Father who art in heaven. Please help me. I don't know what you are doing and why you chose me, but I need you now more than ever. Please protect me and my family and forgive me for any harm that I have caused to anyone. And Father, please never leave me. I need you. I trust you and I am going to let you have your way with my life. In your name…Amen.

I stayed on my knees for an extra moment, letting my thoughts and the prayer marinate. Then, I got up, but I still didn't go to bed. I laid on the couch in the living room, replaying the show over in my head. No matter how many times I recalled every word I'd spoken, it didn't get better.

All I could do was hope and pray that God took care of this. Hours later, after hundreds of replays in my mind, I finally fell into a restless sleep.

The next morning, I got word from my publicist that HARPO reported that the show was their number one watched show so far that year.

"And, JL, they've received thousands of emails," she said, sounding a bit excited until she added, "but not all the emails were good."

"I wonder how Oprah feels about that," I said.

"She's fine. Some people are actually applauding you for bringing this to light. And then the others…well, it doesn't matter. All publicity is good publicity."

But over the next few days, I found out about all the good and the bad. I read articles about how barber shops and beauty salons had come to a stop as everyone was glued to the show. I heard about how it was the hot topic on college campuses.

I was the talk of America—everybody had something to say about the Down Low Brother.

I spent the most time going through my own emails. Talk about the good and the bad, there was a lot of ugly, too. While there were people who applauded me for "coming out" and telling the truth, most didn't have anything good to say about me or what I'd done.

I was called arrogant and egotistical and a pompous ass.

And then, there were all the slurs: I was called a faggot, a punk ass, a tranny.

But even with all of the negativity, it seemed that everyone wanted to read my book. *On The Down Low* didn't officially go on sale until a week after Oprah and it was an instant New York Times Bestseller. People were buying the book, but after reading it, it seemed to fill women with fear. Now, every black man alive was suspected of being on the down low. Women were calling black men shady and sneaky...all because of me. That wasn't my goal when I wrote that book. I was just telling my story.

My story turned into big news. I received even more media requests than I had before. It seemed like every network except for ESPN and the Weather Channel wanted to interview Mr. Down Low. It was overwhelming.

But the most overwhelming part of the experience was the anger that came at me. My gay friends told me about the leaders in the gay community who were pissed off by my testimony.

There were gay men who knew me before I ever appeared on *Oprah*, who were my friends, but now who just wanted to spill my tea. There were rumors that friends and acquaintances were calling newspapers and magazines themselves, trying to sell their stories about me, trying to do everything they could to discredit me.

The hate mail, the hate phone calls, the hate emails continued to build up to the point where I was afraid to even go outside by myself. I stayed in the house for weeks, and then the first time I did go out, I went out in what I considered a disguise: Dark shades, a baseball hat pulled low...and I even shaved off my signature goatee. That may have seemed extreme since Peter and I were only going shopping, but I didn't want to take the chance. I couldn't afford for anyone to recognize me and then go berserk.

It didn't work, though. We went to Marshall Fields in downtown, and while I was walking through the Men's section a couple of women called out my name.

"Oh, my God, it's JL King!"

I looked both ways, ready to run. But then, one of the women shouted, "Wait! Can we take a picture with you?"

When I realized that I wasn't about to be attacked, I relaxed, and did as the women asked; I took photo after photo with them.

"We loved you on the show!" one woman gushed. "We were so proud of you for being so brave!"

As we talked, more people surrounded us, wanting to take their own pictures. By the time I finished, I'd shaken hands, taken pictures and hugged at least fifty people. Once Peter realized that I was surrounded, he came to my rescue and got me out of the store before the crowd became even larger.

As we exited the store, a lady was standing off to the side on her cell phone. "Girl, that brother who was on *Oprah* was at Marshall Fields, and he is fine! I can't believe he's gay. Now, I'm scared to talk to any black man. All of them could be on the down low!"

I was still shaking my head at her comment when Peter and I got into a cab. It seemed that my book had changed the thinking of America and not in a good way. All I could do was pray that this wasn't going to be my legacy.

CHAPTER 23

Jetting to Stardom

*H*ARPO kept replaying the show. I'm not sure how many times they did, but every time my show aired, more requests came in for me to speak. And every time the show aired, the hate emails poured in.

I'm talking about hate mail that included death threats and when I say death threats, I'm not exaggerating. It got to the point where I was afraid to go out even in disguise. So, I had to hire a full-time bodyguard.

But while I was afraid for myself, I was really concerned for my family. At least I had the money and could protect myself, but I hadn't even given my family the benefit of that. Like I said, I didn't share my upcoming book with anyone—not even my father. Thank God my mother wasn't alive to live through this. The humiliation alone would have killed her. So, how could I tell my father that I had a book coming out that told the world I loved men?

So, I hadn't said a word, but I was beginning to really regret that. I knew trouble was coming (I mean, not like this, but I did know there would be trouble.) But I didn't warn my family, I didn't equip them. If I had to do it over again, it would be so different. Then again, my whole life would be different if I were given a chance for a do-over.

But at that time, all I could do was make sure my children and my father were safe. My father lived with my brother at this time, and I didn't see or speak to either one of them too often. I talked to my brother then, though and once I knew they were fine, all I could do for everyone else was pray.

It's important to note that not all the emails were negative; a good portion was positive. But the communication coming to me was so massive, that after a few weeks, I knew that I wouldn't be able to handle it alone. I hired an assistant because I wanted to answer everyone who reached out to me—both the good and the bad. I especially wanted to respond to those sisters who had so many questions. They wanted more information, wanted to know what were the signs, wanted to confirm that they were in a relationship with a straight man... or not.

And then, there were those who wanted to share their stories with me. They wanted to tell me about their experiences with men who *were* on the DL. They wanted my guidance on how to get their men to stop lying. They wanted to understand why a man would put them at risk.

I wanted to reach out to as many people as I could and so months later when I finally felt comfortable going out alone, I spent the year taking on as many speaking engagements as I could. I spoke in five to ten different cities a month, I visited dozens of colleges, I was the keynote for every black woman's organization that would have me.

It was crazy. Every day I received a call from the speakers bureau that was booking me and I really began to embrace what I'd done—how I'd told the world the truth. Yes, it was difficult, but I knew in my heart that I was doing the right thing. I knew that I was answering the call that God had given to me—I was telling my story.

So I continued to speak wherever I was asked to. And then, one of the biggest requests came to me. I received a call from Johnson Publishing Company.

"Mr. Johnson wants you to be interviewed and on the cover of the magazine."

Man, that was huge! To be on the cover of *Jet* Magazine was bigger than being on Oprah—at least to me! I thought about all the icons I'd seen on that cover growing up: Dr. Martin Luther King Jr, Malcolm X, Lena Horne, black leaders in politics, civil rights, and entertainment. You had to be somebody to grace the cover of *Jet* and now, they were asking for me!

Margena Christian, my friend who I'd taken with me to the *Oprah* show, conducted the interview. At the Johnson offices, we talked about DL men and that lifestyle. And for the first time, my children were interviewed about what their lives had been like since the *Oprah* show and the release of my book. Of course, my children just told them that they loved me and that was the beginning and the end for them.

After the interview, we did the photo shoot the next day at the Johnson Building. For the cover, my photos were taken by *Jet's* premiere photographer, who only shot the big covers. It didn't take as long as my photo shoot did for the cover of my book, but I knew the cover for *Jet* would be amazing.

And I was right.

Months later, my cell phone starting blowing up one morning, with calls coming in from family and friends.

"JL! You're on the cover of *Jet*!"

"Oh, my God, you look amazing."

I couldn't wait to see it for myself. I called a friend and asked him to drive me down to the Johnson Publishing building. The publication always mounted the current cover on an easel in the lobby and I wanted to see this for myself.

When I walked into that lobby, I'm telling you, that was a moment I will never forget. There was this huge 36x48 cover of me and right away, the tears welled up in my eyes. I stood there and cried as I thought about my father taking me to the barbershop when I was a kid and seeing all the *Jet* magazines on the table.

Those men in the shop were always talking about the model of the week. And, I used to sit there and admire the beautiful sisters in the swimsuits. Once again, my mind took me to all the famous faces that had graced this cover and all I could do was stand there and cry, taking in the magic of this moment.

When I got myself together, I purchased a couple of dozen copies of the magazine and went back to where my friend waited in his car. I gave him one of the magazines and a smile filled his face.

"Man, you're on *Jet* magazine!" he said like he couldn't believe it. "Now, you're a real celebrity."

That was the thing about *Jet*. While so many people watched *Oprah*, many didn't. But *Jet* magazine was a staple in the black community. In just about every home, you could find *Jet* magazines sprawled across the living room table. This was a really big thing.

That issue became one of their bestselling ones at that time, selling over 85,000 copies in the first week. They had to go back to reprint due to the high demand.

Even though I'd had to deal with so much negativity, I think the *Jet* magazine interview was God's way of sending me reassurance that I had done the right thing. He told me that He was going to make my name great and He was doing just that.

I was really beginning to accept this challenge that God had given to me. My book was necessary. It forced people to have these discussions about sex, sexuality and most importantly HIV. It was needed to get women to really think about how they couldn't give their hearts, their souls and definitely not their bodies to just any man without knowing who he was. My prayer became that this would save the next generation of women from being emotionally destroyed and HIV infected by men who lied.

And the biggest thing about *On the Down Low* was that it forced Black America to start talking about homosexuality in our community. There had been such hatred toward gay black men in our churches, and even in our homes from people who didn't know any better. I wanted to show that these attitudes were what was driving our men into living their secret lives. So while fingers could be pointed at the men who were doing this, there were just as many fingers pointing at our community because we were the reason this was happening.

I no longer felt bad about what I'd written. I hadn't outed a soul, had just exposed my own lifestyle. I wasn't trying to expose any gay men or tell anyone's secrets. This was all about me and using my experiences to help others.

It was amazing that I had to fight so many battles when I was trying to do a good thing. Straight people were upset because I'd brought fear into their lives. Gays were upset because they said I'd written the book only to make money, which clearly wasn't true. The idea for a book never came from me. It came from God.

And when God tells you to do something, you just do it— no matter what the people say.

CHAPTER 24

A Blessing or a Curse?

*T*here were two ways that I could look at my life—I could consider it a curse, or a blessing. There were times when I really felt like it was a curse. All kinds of articles were appearing about me, people were lying saying that they'd had sex with me, saying that I'd stolen money, saying that I'd lied in my book. The Internet bloggers were the cruelest, often bringing my family and friends into their web of hate.

In the beginning, I wanted to address each and every lie that I saw written about me. But people I respected told me to ignore all of that.

"Do you think Oprah responds to any negative thing written about her? You'll end up sitting at your computer sending out emails all day long if you did that," one friend said. "Ignore it. None of those people matter anyway."

So I took that advice and from that day, I haven't paid attention to the lies about me. That was also when I decided to look at my life as a blessing and to take this blessing that I'd been given and do something to help others.

I became a consultant to help people who wanted to publish, and I wanted to write more books as well.

Together, Peter and I wrote *Staying Power,* the unofficial guide for black gay relationships and we published it under the company we created, Chicago Moon Publishing. I didn't put my name on the book; I was just the publisher.

Peter became the face of the book. Our sales were primarily from on-line and to gay groups who brought us in to speak. Peter was really happy about our collaboration and so was I. This was my way of showing him that I truly considered him my partner. It was also my way to contribute financially for the times when Peter had been carrying the entire load himself.

When our book had been out for about six months, I told Peter that it was time for me to get my own condo.

"Why?" he asked, as if he was shocked that I would even consider moving. "What are you talking about?"

"I want Ebony and Brandon to come and visit me," was the line that I gave him.

"They can come here," he said.

I stayed silent, not telling him that I didn't want my children to have to come and stay with me and my lover. It was true that my life was public now, an open book, and my children knew all about me and my lifestyle. But I still didn't want to share my time with anyone when I was being Ebony and Brandon's dad.

Because of my lifestyle, I never saw my children as much as I wanted to when they were growing up. But now that they were grown and in college, I wanted to be there for them as much as I could. It was easier now—now that they completely understood who I was and how I lived. But every chance they got, my children told me that they loved me and that they were proud of me. And I wanted them to know that they were (and had always been) the most important people in the world to me.

But Peter couldn't understand that. Or maybe it was that he didn't want to. He kept asking the same question, "Why do you want to leave me now? You've always had children; we've always worked it out."

Over and over, I tried to explain it to him—this was about my kids. But he wasn't hearing that. Maybe it was because he knew that there was much more to what I was saying. Some of it was about me wanting to get away from him and Peter had to know that.

"Why can't we live together forever?" he asked.

The questions kept on coming, but no matter what he said, or what he did, I just wanted out. Peter was not letting me enjoy this ride that my life had become. He was always on top of me, always watching everything that I did. Maybe it was because he was so jealous. Maybe it was because he was afraid that I would cheat on him. I'd told him that I'd cheated on everybody I'd ever been with; in hindsight, sharing that wasn't my brightest idea. My confession had Peter completely paranoid.

But above his protests, I was going to move out. Without Peter knowing it, I met with a real estate agent who found a really nice, two-bedroom, open-floor layout condo on Wabash, in downtown, exactly where I wanted to be. It was an amazing place, with huge windows that opened up to a view of the lake and Millennium Park. I loved everything about that space and I signed the lease, still without saying a word to Peter.

Since just about everything in the apartment that we shared belonged to Peter, I figured that I would be able to pack up and move my things out one day while he was at work. So that's exactly what I did. One Tuesday morning, the moment Peter closed the door, I jumped up and packed everything I had into my suitcases. I left Peter a note on the kitchen table really trying to explain everything to him. I figured if he had a chance to read it, he would finally understand that I wanted to be a father and I needed my own place so that my children would feel like Chicago was their home, too.

I told him that I would be in contact with him and let him know where I'd moved. Of course I had no plans to do that; I didn't want to hurt him, but I really wanted to end this.

Three days after I moved out, I was living the life. My condo was completely furnished, courtesy of my shopping spree at

Marshall Fields. My favorite piece was my red, Japanese-style, very low-to-the ground sofa.

The walls were stark white, excellent backdrops for the art that I was just beginning to collect. Every day when I walked into that place, I marveled that this was really mine. I loved coming home to my 20th floor apartment. The best way to describe what I felt when I walked inside was...peaceful. And free.

About two weeks after I'd moved, I was on my way out to enjoy the day. I stepped outside, expecting to enjoy this glorious day, but instead I received the shock of my life. Peter was standing right outside the front door. I couldn't believe it; he'd found me.

He stood there, with this look in his eyes that I could only describe as crazy. I could tell that he'd been crying.

Walking over to him, I asked, "How did you find me?"

He started screaming, but he wasn't addressing me. "Hey, everybody! This is where the Down Low Brother lives! This is JL King; don't you all remember him from *Oprah*? He is the man!"

Had Peter had lost his damn mind? He shouted those words over and over to everybody who passed. People started slowing down as they walked down one of the busiest streets in downtown.

"Stop it," I shouted, praying that he would.

But Peter kept going and all I could imagine was someone calling the cops...or worse, the media. I could see the headlines in my mind: *The down low author gets into a fight with his lover in the middle of downtown Chicago.*

That would not be a good look, but the way people were watching now, I knew that could very well happen.

I had to get Peter to calm down, but no matter what I said, or what I did, he got louder. Then finally, he turned his attention directly to me. "What happened? Don't you love me anymore?"

"Peter," I said his name softly, hoping that would diffuse some of his craziness.

"What did I do?" he cried. "I took care of you, I was there for you and now you leave me? All because you wrote a book?"

"Peter!"

"How can you just walk out of my life?"

For a while, people had only slowed down as they passed. But now, folks were actually stopping, gawking at these two men, one crying like a crazy fool.

When a sister pulled out her cell phone, I knew I was in trouble. I didn't know if she was taking pictures or videotaping, but neither one would've been good.

I couldn't stand out there anymore. I had to get Peter away from these inquiring eyes...and cameras.

"Peter, we need to talk. Let's go up to my place."

Just the mention of my place made him quiet down. "Okay," he said, though tears still streamed down his face.

Now instead of screaming, he was whimpering as he followed me inside my upscale building. On the ride in the elevator, all he did was cry. "Why don't you love me anymore? After all I did for you?"

I didn't answer his questions. I just kept saying that we would talk once we got into the apartment. I was relieved when I did get Peter inside. At least none of my neighborhoods would be able to see or hear his foolishness.

Inside my apartment, Peter walked around, checking it out. And the more he walked, the calmer he became.

"This is very nice," he said, as if he hadn't been standing on the street bawling just a few minutes before. "I like it here."

I didn't care if he liked it or not. But still, I said, "Thanks."

"This will work. I can just move in here with you."

Was he kidding me? After all I'd done to get away from him?

I shook my head. "No, that won't work. My kids...Ebony and Brandon...uh...they're going to be staying with me for the summer."

"I don't care!" he shouted. "I'm moving in, dammit!

There was no way that I was ever going to live with Peter again, but I didn't want to deal with this drama for too much longer. So, I told him to sit down and we could talk about it. After about an hour, I had him convinced that he could move in with me. Right after that, I was able to convince him to go home. Because that's what I needed right now—for Peter to get the hell out of my apartment.

As he stood, he said, "You're gonna give me my key?"

"Uh...no. I don't have a spare that I can give to you."

"Then, I'm not leaving!"

I couldn't believe it. I was right back to where I was just a few weeks before. But I didn't have the energy to fight anymore. So, I told Peter about my extra key. "I don't have a spare key that I can give you, but I have one that I leave above the door in case Ebony or Brandon come here and I'm not home."

"Okay, cool," he said, seeming satisfied. "I'll just use that one."

And then, he left without causing any more of a scene. But whether I liked it or not, Peter was definitely back in my life. And short of moving once again, there was nothing that I could do.

Peter began showing up at my condo whenever he wanted to, unannounced as if he were trying to catch me doing something. Because I didn't want his drama, I didn't even have company over, and I didn't date. I never wanted anyone at my home in case Peter showed up. Because if Peter saw me with anyone, he would go ballistic.

So because I didn't have anyone else in my life, before I knew it, I was back in a routine with Peter. Spending most of my time with him and even going to his place, sometimes. I wasn't happy about it, but I didn't know how to get away from him.

Maybe I was as dysfunctional as he was, I don't know. Maybe somewhere inside of me, I thought Peter's drama was his way of letting me know that he loved me. Whatever it was, I felt like I was trapped.

I'd thought about getting a restraining order against him, but I knew that would never keep him away and would only make him angry. I kept hoping that he would change, but the longer we were together, the crazier he got.

We were at his home one night when we got into a major fight. I can't even remember what it was about, but Peter gave me the same ol' lines that he'd always given to me when he got pissed.

"Maybe I should call the media and tell them that you have a boyfriend and we're having problems." Then, he added, "I wonder what Oprah would say finding out that you're a fake ass liar and that you're gay."

Even though those words got under my skin, I always backed down because I never knew if Peter *would* really call the media. Or if he *would* call Oprah.

But on that night, I'd had enough. I was tired of putting up with Peter, tired of being controlled by him, tired of having him in my life. I told him, "Fuck off! I'm leaving."

Peter went straight into his crying routine. "Please don't leave me."

He was still crying when I walked out the door. Then, when I got outside, I heard my name. Turning around, I glanced up, and there was Peter on the balcony, but he was not alone. He was holding our dog over the ledge as if he really intended to drop her five stories down.

"I'm going to drop this bitch if you leave me!"

Even from the street, I could see our puppy trembling with fright. But I was more afraid than our dog. This man was bonafide crazy.

I didn't go back upstairs, though. There was no way that I wanted to deal with crazy tonight. So, I just got into my car and prayed and prayed that he wouldn't drop Mae to her death.

I was still upset when I got home. With what Peter pulled that night, I realized that if I really wanted to get away from Peter, I'd have to leave Chicago. I had wanted to leave for a while anyway. Wanted to get away from the unbearably cold winters, the racially-divided city...and I wanted to get away from crazy.

I began seriously looking into the cities where I'd want to live. Atlanta was the first place that came to mind because from what I knew about that city, it was totally opposite from Chicago. The weather was much milder, black people were running the city, and the cost of living—from food to homes— was far better in the South than the North. I thought that if I could get to Atlanta, I'd have a brand new life!

I know it wasn't just a coincidence that I had a speaking engagement in Atlanta the next week and I ended up staying with a friend who introduced me to his real estate agent. I discovered that for the price that I was paying for my condo, I could have a home in Atlanta. It didn't take much for me to be sold. I was going to move to the ATL.

As soon as I returned to Chicago, I told Peter that I was moving. But to cut down on the drama, I told him that I was moving to Atlanta and I wanted him to come down after I got settled.

"Okay, we can do Atlanta," Peter said, believing that I meant what I said.

For weeks, that lie worked. I packed up my condo, bought a new car, a Porsche and had it shipped to Atlanta, and I was ready to get the hell out of Chicago and away from Peter.

But my lie didn't last long enough. I guess Peter had a chance to think about my move and how it would be much easier for me to disappear from his life once I was out of Chicago. Whatever it was that made him rethink it all, the night before my furniture and belongings were to be shipped to Atlanta, I woke up to the sound of a man whimpering. Before I opened my eyes, I knew it was Peter.

The first thing I did was glance at the digital clock next to my bed. It was a little after one in the morning. Then, I looked up at Peter. He was standing over me, tears pouring from his eyes.

"I'm going to kill you, J. I'm going to kill you if you leave me."

Slowly, I sat up in the bed.

"I'm going to kill you right now if you don't tell me that you're not going to Atlanta."

I believed every word that he said and I jumped out of the bed. I was going to try to make a run for it, even though I was butt-naked, but I couldn't move fast enough. He grabbed me, swung me around and with his hand, put a chokehold on my dick.

"I love you," Peter cried.

Since I couldn't get away, I had to think of something else. So, I said, "I love you, too."

"Do you really?" he said, releasing me.

"Yes," I said. "But I really need you to leave so that I can get some sleep."

"No," he responded and grabbed me again. "I'm not leaving until you tell me that you're going to stay here."

"Of course, I'm going to stay," I told him even though there were U-Haul boxes stacked high all around us. "I would never leave you and if you don't want to go to Atlanta, then I'll just cancel the move and you can move in with me right here."

He was crying so hard, nose-running and all. But, I had to keep talking to get this crazy fool out of my home. Slowly, we walked together toward the front door. I had a plan already in my head: I was going to get him close enough where I could push him out, lock the door, then call 9-1-1. I didn't have to worry about him acting any crazier if I called the police. By the time he got out of jail, I'd be out of Chicago.

This was a plan that had to work because I was sure that Peter was crazy enough on this night to really do me harm, and maybe even kill me.

I imagined the headlines would read: The Down Low Brother found dead in downtown high rise. Murdered by his male lover. I thought about all the people who would rejoice at that news.

I kept talking and the more I talked, the more Peter let me lead him. We were getting closer and closer to the point where I could execute my plan. A couple of seconds later, we were right there. At the door. I reached for the door's knob at the same moment that Peter reached for one of the African walking sticks that I kept in an umbrella stand. It happened so quickly, but slow enough for me to see every move that Peter made.

He pulled up one of the bigger sticks from the stand, leaned back, and with all of his might hit me upside my head. All of his two hundred and forty pound strength was behind that blow, and I stumbled back to the wall. Right away, I felt the blood and before I hit the floor, I thought...what a crazy way to die!

⤬

"Oh, my goodness! Mr. King? Mr. King?"

I recognized my neighbor's voice, but I couldn't open my eyes. Couldn't even lift my head, so forget about standing up and going into my room so that I could put on some clothes.

"Mr. King, you stay right there," my neighbor said, as if I *could* move. "I'm gonna call the police."

I felt her movements as she rushed to my phone and slowly, my senses came back to me. She was talking to 9-1-1 by the time I was able to open my eyes. And finally, I pushed myself up.

"Oh, no," she ran back to me, "don't move. The ambulance is on its way. And the police."

I groaned.

"Are you okay, Mr. King? Please don't try to move."

My head hurt like nothing I'd ever felt before. I needed to get up, get dressed, but every time I moved my head, I saw stars. I was still sitting there, leaning against the wall and butt-naked when the EMTs and police arrived at the same time.

"Thank God you're here," my neighbor said.

As the paramedics, examined my wound, I heard the policeman ask my neighbor what happened.

"I don't know," she said. "I heard this loud thump on the wall and I jumped out of my bed it scared me so much. I thought it came from the hallway, and when I opened my door to check it out, I saw this man running toward the stairs and Mr. King's door was open. That's when I found him lying there. I thought he was dead!"

The EMTs had slipped me onto the stretcher by the time the policeman turned his attention to me. "So you were attacked?" the officer asked.

What was I supposed to say? Now that I thought about it, I didn't want the police involved. If I turned on Peter, he would tell them that I was his boyfriend, his lover. And if that news got out, the world might think that I was actually gay.

But before I could make up a story, one of the paramedics said, "He's not going to be able to talk to you right now. We have to take him in."

I had never been so grateful as I was rolled away. This would give me time to come up with some kind of cover story.

On the ride to the hospital, the paramedics kept asking me questions as if they wanted to keep me talking.

"Do you know what day it is?"

"Who's the president?"

"Where do you live?"

By the time I arrived at the hospital, I was fully alert and felt much better, but after the doctors checked me out, they decided to keep me in the ER for a few hours.

"You're not going to need any stitches," the doctor told me as he examined my forehead.

"I'm not? But there was so much blood."

"Yes, any cut from the scalp will bleed like that, but mostly, you just have swelling."

I reached up and felt my forehead. It felt like it had quadrupled in size.

"So, I'm going to be okay?"

"I think so. I just want this swelling to go down a bit before we have you up and walking."

"Okay."

"You know, you're very lucky. You could have died; many people die from blunt force trauma."

I knew it! Peter was truly trying to kill me. I had to get away from his crazy ass. "So, how long am I going to be in here?"

"Just a few hours. If there are no complications, I'll have you checked out of here by noon." And then, as if to further emphasize what I already knew, the doctor said once again, "You're very lucky."

As soon as he stepped away, I grabbed the hospital phone. I wasn't sure if it was going to work, but I guess since I was making a local call, it did.

"Hello, Mrs. Peterson," I said to Peter's grandmother.

"Jimmy, is that you?" she said, almost sounding like she was expecting my phone call even though it was in the middle of the night. "Are you all right?"

"Yes, I was calling...."

"I know," she said, without letting me finish. "Peter called and told me what happened. He told me what he did. I'm so sorry, Jimmy."

So he had called his grandmother and told her that he had tried to kill me?

"Are you all right?" she asked again.

"The doctor said I'm lucky, that I could've died."

"I'm so sorry."

"And the police want to know what happened."

"You didn't tell them, did you?" she asked, sounding frantic.

So much of me wanted to say that I had. I wanted Peter to suffer for all that he'd put me through.

She begged, "Please don't press charges. You know Peter's not well."

Who was she telling?

"You know he has that bi-polar thing."

Bi-polar thing?

"You know that, right? I've been trying to get him to see a doctor and get medication. Maybe now he will. But please don't press charges; please don't have him sent to jail."

All along I'd known that Peter had issues; I just didn't know the extent.

"Don't worry, Mrs. Peterson. I won't press charges," I said more for her and me, than for Peter. I really wanted him to pay. But then, his family would suffer, and I would suffer, too.

"Oh, thank you, thank you, thank you." She was still thanking me when I hung up the phone.

Peter was lucky—he had two things going for him: his grandmother whom I really loved, and the police who never came to the hospital to question me anymore. I guess there was too much going on in Chicago to get involved with a guy who ended up with a bump on his head.

Even though it was four in the morning, I called a good friend of mine, told him what had happened with Peter and asked him to go to my apartment and bring me some clothes, my cell phone, and my wallet. Like the doctor promised, I was released at noon.

My friend had gone back to my apartment to let the movers in at nine and by the time I got home, everything was on its way to Atlanta.

Originally, I wasn't supposed to officially leave Chicago until the next day, but I changed my ticket, paying a premium price. I didn't care if it cost me a million dollars—I wanted out of that city.

Just eight hours after I'd been released from the hospital, I was on a plane, hovering high. I looked out the window and said a silent goodbye. I would never regret coming to Chicago; after all, many great things happened to me there. But, I'd never been so happy to leave a place. Never in my life.

Years later, I found out that Peter checked himself into a mental hospital after he attacked me. He had a breakdown that almost cost me my life. But I never heard from him for many, many years, and I was able to begin life anew in Atlanta. I was able to leave crazy behind in the Windy City.

CHAPTER 25

The New Chocolate City

*I*t didn't take me long to say—I love Atlanta! When I got to the new chocolate city, I checked into an upscale hotel. That was going to be my residence while I house-hunted.

I searched for a home in Midtown. I wanted a big house where I could spread out and enjoy the community that was filled with restaurants, bars, and Piedmont Park.

My real estate agent, a black women, showed me several homes outside of Atlanta, but I wanted an Atlanta address— not something out in the suburbs. When I told people that I lived in Atlanta, I wanted to say it and mean it. I wanted to be in the city.

Finally, she found me the perfect place—a million dollar home in the heart of Midtown. It was in a gated community of only thirty homes. Though the homes were spectacular, there wasn't a lot of land, and there was no front yard at all.

But I loved the four-level home in the cluster community with its huge windows and great views. The porch wrapped around the first floor and the lower level had an outdoor Jacuzzi. It was love at first sight; I wanted that home...and I got it.

Atlanta was known for its show and tell lifestyle; it was all about big homes and fancy cars. I wanted to keep up with that, live above the norm, live large. So once I closed on my million dollar crib, I purchased a Range Rover to add to my Porsche. Then, I hired a full time housekeeper, a chef, a gardener (even though I didn't have much of a yard) and a dog sitter for when I had to travel (since I'd gotten my own dog.) I also added three full-time personal assistants, a car service (I really didn't like to drive even though I had purchased two cars) and a security guard to my staff.

Just weeks after arriving, I was the "it" boy in the city. I threw lavish parties and invited the Who's Who of Atlanta as my guests. Everyone wanted to get next to me, to be in my circle. I had my pick of men *and* women. It didn't matter. They all wanted to be connected to JL King.

Of course, I got connected in the gay community, too. Atlanta, being the gay capital of the country, always had a party going on somewhere. And these parties were equivalent to red carpet events. Each host tried to outdo the next one, so these events were all spectacular.

But even though I loved to party, I still wasn't comfortable being around a lot of gay men. I still wasn't gay, you know, so I always attended, but only made short appearances. And I'd always attend with a couple of my inner circle friends. At these parties, I wouldn't talk to anyone except my boys. If someone wanted to chat or take a picture with me, I'd do it, but not for very long. And after a few hours, I'd just leave. Without saying goodbye to anyone.

But though I didn't hang out at parties, my sex life exploded in Atlanta. Talk about being a kid in the candy store—brothers were lining up to sleep with me and I didn't turn many down. I was sleeping with so many guys that I couldn't remember names or faces after a while.

I began to develop a reputation as a player and a whore after several of the brothers that I sexed decided they wanted more. They wanted to move in and play house—they wanted a relationship. But I wasn't interested in anything beyond the sex. Once I had that, I was ready to move on.

It was a fabulous life. I was still on my extensive book tour, still doing lots of media and speaking, still traveling most of the time. But I always loved being home, though the celebrity life never stopped. Not even when I was inside of my home.

One day when I was out walking my dog, a tour bus was parked outside of the gate. When I stepped out onto the street, a couple of women yelled out to me.

"Hey, Down Low Brother! We wanted to see where you lived."

I couldn't believe it. Atlanta tour buses had me on their circuit now?

"Can we take a picture with you?" one asked.

Another one said, "I have my book with me. I know you'll sign it, right?"

They piled off the bus, about four or five of them. After taking the pictures, I was signing everything—their books, even copies of the *Jet* magazine.

And while we chatted, they asked the question that sisters all over the country asked me. "What are the signs? How can I know if my man is on the down low?"

I sighed. If I had just a penny for every time I was asked that question, I would have more money than Donald Trump!

CHAPTER 26

A Faith-Filled Man

I believe in God. Period. I am a man of faith. Another period. Many people don't know that, or believe that, but I don't care. I don't have to explain my faith to anyone because there is only One who can save me.

But just because I have faith, just because I love The Lord doesn't mean that I haven't made a ton of mistakes. It's that free will thing—God gives us free will and He's not going to interfere with our decisions. And sometimes, I think that's too bad because I've made some really bad decisions in my life where I wish that He'd stopped me.

And the way I was living in Atlanta was one of those bad decisions. I had a $4,500/month mortgage, an employee payroll of $10,000 a month, a $500,000 condo in Chicago and I bought anything I wanted, any time I wanted. Everything from clothes, to jewelry, to exotic trips. It went on and on and on. I did all of that even though Uncle Sam's cousin, Uncle IRS was on my ass like a pimp.

But it's important to note that I wasn't just spending my money on me. I gave away money to charities and various organizations, especially HIV prevention centers. I lent money to friends who treated me like their personal ATMs and I gave money to strangers, especially homeless mothers or any single mother who told me she needed help feeding her children. That was the heart that God had given to me. I'd always wanted to be a helper, a giver and I was grateful to be in the position to help.

But it got out of control, and I was foolish in the way I was spending money. I was acting out what most people believed—that since I was on *Oprah* and she endorsed my book, I was a multi-millionaire and now I had endless money. Listen up—I did not become a millionaire. Yes, I made quite a bit of money with Oprah's help and for that, I will always be grateful. But a millionaire, I am not and was not back then, though I was acting that way.

I had to find my way back and I knew the only road to take was with God. I'd lost Him in all the hype. I was living way too big. It got to the point where I felt like I was really screwing up and losing control of my life. I was only spending money because I wanted to maintain this facade. I was in the public eye and people thought that I was more that I really was and that I had more than I really had.

It was killing me, maintaining that front. I felt nothing but pressure, and felt as if I was spiraling out of control. It was hard, too, because I had no one to turn to. The men in my life were really just dudes that I was having sex with. They depended on me, I couldn't depend on them. And the women were nothing more than groupies; I couldn't call any of them friends. Hell, I was even having sex with a few of them! Yes, women who knew my story, women who knew that I was having sex with men still wanted to have sex with me and I wasn't going to turn down any offer. It was amazing to me—all the women. Women who thought they could change me, women who told me that once I had sex with them, I would never go back to men.

Yeah, right! I sexed anyone who let me since at this point in my life I was upfront with everyone. Yes, I will have sex with you, but I'm going to have sex with everyone else, too—men and women.

Still, it didn't matter. Women saw the same thing in me that men saw—I was a successful author, good-looking, living this grand lifestyle. Everyone wanted to be the last one standing as my partner.

With the way my life was going, I knew that I had to get back into prayer mode, recommit my life to God, and ask for His guidance.

I found a church, on the far southwest side of Atlanta, Word of Faith, under the leadership of Bishop Dale Bronner, from the famous Bronner family. The Bronners have a hair care empire and Dale was the minister of the family.

Word of Faith was one of those mega churches. Three services with more than ten thousand people attending each. I didn't make any announcement to the church that I was going to be attending. It wasn't about that for me, I didn't want that kind of attention. I was there to worship, and get the Word of God.

I knew Word of Faith was the right place for me because at every service I praised, and then, I cried. I attended the services with the current man that I was seeing and both of us were getting fed by the bishop.

One Sunday, this sister recognized me as I was leaving. "Are you JL King?" she asked, stopping me. Before I could answer, she said, "Oh, my God. I love your books. Are you a member here?"

"No, I just love the services."

"You need to tell Bishop Bronner so that you can get the VIP treatment and sit up front." Then, she whispered, "You know a lot of celebrities go to this church."

She was telling the truth. I'd seen them—actors, musicians, directors. But honestly, I didn't want all of that. I wanted the worship, that was the main thing.

But I also didn't want to say anything to the pastor because my reputation wasn't exactly church friendly. To most, I was still the DL brother who had lied to his wife. Among many Christians, there was no forgiveness for me. It didn't matter that I'd told the truth now. It didn't matter that what I said now was actually saving lives. It didn't matter that God had forgiven me—they were not going to forgive. In their eyes, once a liar, always a liar and the truth would never be within me.

So, I knew that I would be judged by the members, even though the choir stand was full of gay men that I personally knew. Some of them were even married. I'd had a few of those encounters—walking in or out of the church, seeing a man walk in with his wife and children, him seeing me, and then turning to stone.

But all I ever did was say 'hello' and keep it moving. I wasn't ever going to call out anyone or blow their cover. There were times when I wanted to because I was thinking of the women. After what I'd done to Brenda and the women I dated after my divorce, I wanted all women to be given the choice. The women had a right to know that their man was sexing a man and then they could decide to stay or leave.

But, I never said a word, never told a thing. Like I said, my only purpose for coming to this church was God. I needed Him to find my center. I needed to get back to the place where God was the head of my life. Where I told Him that I loved Him daily. Where I knew that He loved me.

Interestingly enough, it was at Word of Faith where I got back to God and finally accepted who I was.

I was a gay, black man!

That had always been so hard for me to say, so hard to accept, so hard for me to believe. Maybe some of that had to do with my upbringing in the church. I'd always heard that if you were a homosexual, you couldn't possibly love God.

Well, I certainly loved Him and I knew Him. So, no way was I gay.

But Bishop Bronner gave me another perspective. He never gay-bashed, and I came to really accept who I was. I realized that I was a helpless man who was in need of a Savior, and being gay didn't change that. Now, I realize that there are many who don't believe that a gay person can be saved, but here is what I know—God made me this way because I came out of my mother's womb like this. How else can you explain me being nine years old and putting my cousin's penis in my mouth? I wasn't taught that, I'd never seen that. It was a desire that had been rising inside of me and at nine, before I really knew anything about sex, I acted upon an impulse that I didn't understand.

The only explanation for what I'd done at the age of nine is that I was born that way. And that means the God who made me like this, accepts me like this.

I once heard a woman I really respect say that she agreed with me, but not in the way I thought. She said that we were made this way, just as she'd been made—we all came into this world as sinners and homosexuality was my sin, just like she had her sins. But she said that God loved me, just like He loved her. Except that she encouraged me to fight through my sin, just like she fought through hers.

Maybe that's true, maybe it's not. All I know for a fact, all I can tell you is that I love The Lord with all of my heart. I no longer debate it or try to get other people to understand or believe me. I just know that there are parts of my life that God doesn't approve of—especially having all this sex without the benefit of marriage—but there are parts of my life that pleases Him. And I know that He approves of me telling my story—through my books and my speaking engagements—because He was the one who told me to do that twelve years ago.

It was Word of Faith and Bishop Bonner who finally allowed me to accept all of that. I did all I could to keep God first and stay in touch with Him. That is never easy, but I tried to do everything I could to maintain my relationship with God.

CHAPTER 27

I Want Love, Too!!!

*M*aybe it was because I finally really accepted who I was that made me want to change my life. I wanted love, I wanted to be in a real relationship. With a man. No cheating involved, no cheating accepted.

Truly, I was tired of the Internet dating scene. Yes, those Internet sites gave me all the sex I needed, all over the country, at any time. But those sites never gave me what I wanted—love.

The challenge was though, how could I meet someone and be sure that they were into me and not all the celebrity stuff that came with me? Was it possible for me to meet someone who didn't care about JL, and the DL Brother, and the *Oprah* Show and the book and everything else? Was it possible for me to meet someone who would just love Jimmy King?

One night when I was hanging out with about nine male friends, I started telling them about how I really wanted to find a partner, settle down and be in a relationship for the rest of my life. I told them that I wanted love and I wanted to give love.

My words truly came from my heart, so when one of my friends said, "Who do you think would want to be with you?" I was really insulted.

But, he went on to explain, "You're rich, you're a celebrity, you're too well-known, you have a reputation as a playboy and on top of all of that, you're bigger than life. You're not the average dude that just anybody can date."

Clearly, that was not the response I expected nor wanted. "Why would you say that?" I asked him.

"Everybody knows JL King! So how is a guy gonna get with you and take you to their friends' house? Or worse, how is he going to take you to church? And you know what? Church might not be the worst part—how is this guy gonna tell his family that he's dating you?" He shook his head like he was an expert. "No, it would cause too much debate and conversation. It's never gonna happen."

His words hurt, but I knew he was telling the truth.

"I do have a suggestion, though." He paused and I listened, thinking he was about to give me some great words of advice. "You can always go incognito. The next guy you meet, don't tell him who you are." He laughed. "As if there's one person in America who doesn't know you."

My boys all laughed, but I didn't. I began thinking...maybe that was the way to find true love. Maybe if guys didn't know who I was, I would know that they were into me for me. We could get to know each other first, fall in love, then I could reveal my true identity. And all would be well.

So, I left the club that night thinking that my friend had said those words as a joke, but I was going to see if I could make it work.

It didn't take me long to put it to the test. I ran into this guy at Starbucks, and I really liked the way we vibed. He told me his name was Rob; I told him my name was Jimmy. That wasn't a lie, but that was the only thing that I told him about me that was close to the truth. Everything else I made up—I told him that I used to be a teacher, but was between jobs right now and that I was born and raised in Chicago.

After that first meeting at Starbucks, we talked every day for a week, and after that, got together to go for long walks with our dogs. When we weren't going for walks, we'd hang out at his apartment. I'd never invite him to mine, always making the excuse that I wasn't a good housekeeper.

"I don't care about that," he'd say. "I want to see where you live."

But I was able to convince him that his house was always the better place to hang out. And it was, because there was too much JL King stuff hanging around at my house.

I was really feeling Rob and as the weeks passed, I began thinking that there was going to come a time when I'd want to tell him the truth about me. I felt that I was close to being able to do that now; Rob was into me as much as I was into him. He liked me for the right reasons. Now, all I had to do was tell him who I really was and hope that he really accepted me.

We'd been hanging for a couple of months when he said, "We need to go out."

"What are you talking about? We go out all the time." Even though I said that, I knew what Rob meant. He wanted to go out-out. Be out in public. Yes, we hung outside all the time, but I was careful not to go to places where I thought we might run into folks who knew me. So, I kept our outside encounters to walks in the park, and Starbucks.

"I want to take you some place special. To my favorite restaurant. They have this special on Tuesday nights—lobster tails."

We both loved seafood, so I was up for that—except, I was a bit apprehensive about being out in public like that. But I talked myself out of that, determined not to be afraid. Atlanta wasn't some small country town. This was a big city. It wasn't like we were definitely going to run into someone that I knew.

So when he picked me up that evening, I put all the negative thoughts out of my mind. On the way to the restaurant, we jammed to the old school music that was on the radio. For me, that was a good sign—this was going to be a good night.

Inside the restaurant, I did a quick scan as the hostess led us to our table. I was relieved; there was no one in there that I recognized. We were seated near a table of about eight women, who appeared to be having a some kind of celebration.

I relaxed. It seemed that our first time really out in public was going to be great. That was when I decided that it was time to be honest with Rob. I was ready for our relationship to go further.

We selected our wine, ordered dinner, and as we chatted, I noticed a couple of the women at the table next to us, eyeing me. That was when I started sweating. My prayer was they were just trying to get a better glimpse of a good-looking brother. But then when one of them stood and began walking toward our table, I realized that my prayer wasn't going to be answered.

"I just wanted to say that I loved your book," the woman said as she stood over our table. "It really helped me get over an ugly relationship and I wanted to come over and thank you."

"You're welcome," I said, hardly able to get the words out.

She said, "Would you mind if we got a picture with you? It's my girl's birthday and it would mean a lot to us."

From the corner of my eye, I could see Rob staring with a 'What the hell?' look on his face. Without giving him a single explanation, I stood, and took the photos, though I kept my chatting to a minimum. I had to get back to Rob.

When I returned to our table, Rob barely let me sit down before he said, "Who are you, bro, and what were they talking about a book you wrote?"

It was the anger that I heard in his voice that made me take a deep breath before I told him what I had planned to tell him anyway. "I'm JL King. I wrote that book about brothers on the down low."

He looked at me as if he'd never seen me before.

"Have you heard about that book?" I asked.

"Yeah," he said. "I've heard a few things. But why didn't you tell me? Why did you lie?"

"Because. . ."

He didn't even give me a chance to finish. "You know what? It doesn't matter." He pushed back his chair, threw his napkin on the table and stood. "I don't like games and I don't like people playing with me."

"That's not what I was doing."

"I never lied to you about anything, but if you can't even be honest about your name, about who you are...you and I don't need to know each other. I don't need anyone in my life like that."

"Rob, it wasn't like that."

He shook his head as if he felt sorry for me. "You're fucked up, you know that, right? I'm out."

Then, he just walked away. Literally. He walked out of the restaurant leaving me with the bill and no way to get home.

Not only was I crushed, but I also felt like a damn fool. Rob was right; I had played him, though that wasn't my intent. All

I wanted was for someone to like me, to love me without that JL King brand being part of the situation and their decision.

I paid the bill, then hailed a cab and cried on the ride all the way home. I felt dejected, not only at losing Rob, but I felt like this was what my future was going to look like. I was going to grow old, all alone.

After a few days of feeling sorry for myself, my thoughts turned back to the Internet. Maybe that was all my life was destined to be—relationships with men who didn't give a damn about my name. Maybe all I was ever going to have were encounters with men who wanted no conversation, just a few hours of sex and then they would be gone. Men who wanted no follow-ups, no numbers exchanged, no expectations. Just in and out.

So, I decided to go back to my old ways. But then, Steven walked into my life.

⟨≈⟩

I was just about to hit the Internet hard when I met Steven. He was just my type: light-skinned with curly hair, gorgeous hazel eyes and a seriously tight body. He was a very successful and popular radio host and part of the elite of Atlanta.

And, he was in the closet. He wasn't on the DL, he wasn't in a relationship, but he was not out—at least not all the way. Of course, those in the gay community knew he was gay. But it wasn't public knowledge, though he wasn't afraid of being seen with me.

When we started dating, it was good. We were all over Atlanta together—at parties, dinners at the finest restaurants, attending concerts, plays and red carpet events, always having the best front row seats. He even acted as my publicist when I needed to have one nearby.

And then there was our physical relationship—the sex was off the chain!

What was best about Steven was that he was proud to be my partner and I think that was because while he was proud of me and what I'd done, he considered himself my equal. So, he was happy that we were together and he let everyone know it. We became one of the city's power gay couples—at least inside the gay community.

But Steven was like me. He didn't like to be around gay people too much. So we had a lot of straight friends, especially females who would hang out at my home or his condo in Buckhead.

Our weeks of dating turned into months that became a year, and I was sure that I'd finally found it. The long-term, forever and ever relationship that I'd been hoping for. There was just one thing about Steven that challenged me. And it was a big thing—he was an addict. He would never admit it, but he had a serious drinking and drug problem.

I hadn't really noticed it at first because a lot of gay men like to party hard on drugs and liquor. It's something I noticed back in the first years when I would hang out with gay men.

I think the alcohol and drugs were used to medicate the pain that these men were carrying.

It wasn't until I'd been with Steven for about a year that I noticed how much he really drank. He downed Patron like water, spending hundreds of dollars every few days on liquor. And he was a sloppy drunk, wanting to argue and fight with me when I wouldn't let him drive after he'd spent $250 on drinks.

When I wasn't with him, Steven would drive and in less than a few months, he had six DUIs. But even that didn't scare him. He felt he was above the law.

During our second year together, I cannot tell you how many times I had to bail Steven out of the Fulton and Cobb county jails. I tried to get him help, I really did. But whenever I told him that I wanted him to get help, he told me that he didn't have a problem.

"I just like to party," Steven said all the time. "You're making too much of this. Just because you don't drink, you think everyone is a drunk."

So, he kept spending money, and he kept getting arrested, and he kept pushing me away. I loved Steven because when he was sober, we vibed so well. He was witty and always full of good conversation—everything from entertainment to politics. And he was kind and gentle and only wanted to be with me, James King. That was what he called me - James. Not JL. He didn't care about any of that. We never talked about my books nor the brand that I had become. And it wasn't in a disrespectful way. He was proud of who I was and what I accomplished, but he said none of that had anything to do with who we were as a couple. He had his own success, so when we were together, it was just about him and me. He wasn't interested in any part of my life that wasn't about us. That was so refreshing to me.

I wanted it to work with Steven, but the more money he spent on getting high, the more times he got arrested, the more he made me want to walk away. He was pushing me out of the relationship.

It came to a head when one night we were entertaining friends at his condo and Steven was so ugly-drunk that he started a fight with one of our guests. He was cursing and drooling all over himself before he passed out.

I was embarrassed, actually humiliated and that was when I knew I couldn't stay any longer. All of those years with him, but I had to get out or Steven was going to destroy me along with himself.

Of course, I couldn't just walk away. Couldn't just say that I wanted out. No, I had to get out the only way I knew how. I had to revert to what I knew best—so, I cheated on Steven. I went back to what I'd done from my first relationship, my marriage...I had an affair.

It was easy to meet my new partner—I met him while cruising one of the gay sites. Charles Wilson, a schoolteacher who lived close to my home.

I contacted him and invited him over for sex. He was my type and the sex was great. But afterward, we started talking and he ended staying up all night talking about his work with youth. He didn't know I was JL King. To him I was just a dude off the street, or should I say off the site.

Our encounter didn't end with that one night, though. I liked talking to Charles, so I invited him over again, several times. And we would laugh and talk and eat popcorn in bed while watching TV. I don't know how it happened or why, but after a few months of hanging out, I fell in love with him. Now mind you, I wasn't totally out of my relationship with Steven, though I wanted out. And I especially wanted out now that I'd met Charles who was so sane compared to Steven.

Of course I wasn't honest with Steven or Charles. Steven obviously didn't know that I was cheating. And Charles didn't know that I was in a relationship.

So, I just kept on with life that way until Charles did to me what I'd done to other people—he just moved on. He wasn't looking for anything permanent. He just wanted sex.

I was hurt, and because I didn't want to be alone, I stayed with Steven. But it was hell at home. Steven's addiction was becoming worse and really, there was nothing that I could have done to save him or our relationship. As long as a bottle of Tequila was more important to Steven than I was, it was never going to work.

Eventually Steven and I stopped having sex, and you knew it was over then. That made it easier to walk away.

But once I did, I had to again question myself—would I ever be able to find true love? Or would it always be out of reach for me? And if I found it, would I be able to change my behavior? Would I ever be able to stop cheating on the people that I professed to love?

I posed this question to one of my friends and he laughed.

"J, you will always be a cheater. It's in your DNA." And then, he laughed some more.

I needed to stop asking my friends for advice because every time I did, I got my feelings hurt. But the thing was, what he said was true. I'd been cheating so long that I wondered if I would ever change, could I ever change? Or was it a habit now that would be impossible to break?

I prayed then and I pray now that my friend was wrong. Because I truly do want to find love. I am blessed; my life is filled with the love of my children and my grandson, but there is still a place in my heart that fears growing old alone. I guess, though, that is one of the consequences of the life that I've chosen to live.

That will never stop me from dreaming of the day when I'll be able to have a partner, and introduce him to my friends and bring him home to my family. I want the man I love to be able to celebrate holidays and special occasions with those that I love. I want to be able to create a life with a man like my ex-wife was able to create with her new husband—a life that blessedly includes me.

CHAPTER 28

We Are Family

Brenda Marie Stone, my ex-wife and I have a bond that will never end. Yes, I hurt her and I will always be sorry for that, but I am grateful because time has a way of truly healing even deep emotional wounds.

It took some time for Brenda to get past the hurt and deal with the issues that I'd created. But over time, she was able to forgive me. She did it privately, and she did it publicly when she appeared with me on the *Oprah* show for my second appearance.

But here's what's so special about my ex-wife. Even while she was still reeling from the hurt I had caused with my behavior, she wanted our children to have both of their parents in their lives. It would've been very easy for her to keep our son and daughter away from me. But she didn't. She thought about our children first, knowing that it was better for them to have both parents, better for them to know that they had the love of their mother and their father.

She was never going to allow my instability to mess up their stability and so she never dogged me nor talked about me nor became the "Angry Black Woman" who wanted to kill me. She never got on television nor the radio nor any newspaper to bad-mouth me. Not that she didn't have offers. You know everyone wanted to get to the down low brother's ex-wife. And she was getting plenty of advice, too. From strangers who told her all kinds of ways to cause me harm and who even advised her of ways that she could "remove my penis from my body."

But what these people never knew was that Brenda would never exhibit that kind of behavior; she was far too classy for that. She was raised by Mr. and Mrs. Stone, who taught all of their children to walk with their heads high at all times, even if they were hurting inside.

So that's what Brenda did. She held her head high, allowed me to be in my children's life (though she cut off every other tie to me.) And because she had an open heart, she was able to find love for herself once again. This time, she found true love with a wonderful man who has given her everything that I wasn't able to give. He's given her the life that she deserves.

I will always be grateful to Brenda and her husband, not only for forgiving me, but for providing my children with a wonderful environment to grow. Brenda has given them the same kind of home that she tried to provide for me—a home filled with warmth and love and most importantly, God.

And what's simply amazing is that she's opened that home to me. Once Brenda remarried, I was concerned about my place in my children's lives. Brenda knew that I would never accept being on the outside looking in and I told her that I still wanted to be part of the family, especially during holidays and family gatherings. Of course she had to talk to her husband and I respected that. But the two of them accepted me into their home and to this day, we spend time together...as a family. We sit together and talk and laugh and pray...as a family.

Some may see this as very strange. Many people would find it impossible to have this type of gathering at their home. But this is one of the testimonies that I pray comes out of my life's example. In our community, we talk about our love for Christ, but forgiveness is something that we often don't embrace. The thing is though, forgiveness is a powerful spirit and when you keep God first, anything is possible. Because it is only with God's grace that I was forgiven and I have this relationship with my ex-wife and her husband.

Now there is one caveat, though. While I am welcomed, I have never felt comfortable showing up to our family dinners with my boyfriend. I've talked to Brenda and my daughter about doing that some time, and the idea didn't go over well with either of them—for obvious reasons.

So even though all of these years have passed, I have never once brought a man around my family. I could press the issue, but honestly, I don't think I'd feel comfortable. I've never had my children around any man and I guess, there's no reason for me to change now. At least not until I find the one that I will be with for the rest of my life.

But one day, I will show up with my man. Not out of disrespect, but because I think it's important. I know my children want me to be happy and finding that man will make me happy. Once I find him, I will want to share everything with him, including my family.

I also think it's important because I truly want our community to see that love is love. And maybe this example will help just one man who's living in the closet to come out and live his truth—especially if he sees that he can maintain his relationship with his children.

That's what it's always been about for me. My kids. And I thank God that Brenda is the type of woman who never made me fight for a relationship with Ebony and Brandon.

I am blessed, but there are many gay men who are not where I am. And that's because of society. I've gotten to this place in my life where I don't care what people think about me or how I live my life. It's so much easier when you realize that opinions are like buttholes, everybody has one.

But while that's allowed me to be free, not every gay man can say that. Society has called gay men all kinds of names, and claimed that gay men have all kinds of perversions. I've read where some have stated that gay men shouldn't be allowed to be fathers, and they definitely shouldn't be allowed to be alone with their children because after all, aren't all gay men pedophiles? Won't they try to turn their children out?

Where people get this from, I will never know. Let's all agree on something right here and right now. Pedophilia is an illness that has nothing to do with being gay. The majority of gay men, like straight men, do not want to have sex with children. I've had so many of my gay friends ask me to use my national platform to tell the world that. One gay man shared this story with me.

The Story of Alex Hamilton:

I have four children: two boys, ages 10 and 12, and a set of baby twin girls. After my wife and I divorced, I wanted to take my sons on a camping trip. We were going with my boyfriend and he was also bringing his two sons.

My sons were excited; I had planned a full weekend of father-son time. We were going fishing and hiking and horseback riding. They were so happy, and of course, shared the upcoming adventure with their mother.

The night that I told my sons about it, I got a frantic phone call from my wife.

"I am not going to let you take *my* sons around another gay man. And on a camping trip where no one can watch you? That's not gonna happen."

I told her, "I'm taking *my* sons on this trip; they want to go and we're going!"

We went back and forth, the argument heating up.

My ex-wife said, "I don't want my sons being molested by you and your sick faggot friends!"

Her words shocked me. And then she hung up the phone.

I jumped into my car, drove over to her house where the argument continued.

She said, "I don't trust you around my sons."

"They're my sons, too."

"I don't care what you say; I'm not letting you take them so that your faggot friends can molest them!"

I couldn't believe that she repeated what she'd said over the phone, but standing there in front of her, I could tell that she was serious.

"What are you talking about? I'm not a pedophile and neither are any of my friends. You need to get your facts straight."

"I have my facts straight. My pastor told us that gay men shouldn't be around children."

She went on to say that the pastor had told the congregation that gay men didn't need to be around children because they would try to turn them into homosexuals.

I just couldn't believe that my wife believed that, but she did. I had to cancel the trip, but my wife and I ended up in court. Even though I'd lost the battle to take my sons on a camping trip, I won the war when the judge told my wife that what I did with my children on my court ordered visits had nothing to do with her as long as the children were not in danger. And that if she couldn't prove that my sons were being molested, then the next time she tried to stop me from seeing them, she would be arrested.

That was a court order, but still my wife was not happy. She told my sons to be careful and that, "If anything is not right with your father or his friends, you tell me."

Of course, everything was fine, but she still planted seeds inside of my son's minds. She wanted them to believe that my friends and I were sick, that there was something terribly wrong with us....

When I heard Alex's story, I was pissed off. But then, it was hard for me to stay angry with the mother. She felt that way because of her lack of knowledge and because she'd been brainwashed by the church. The church that has labeled homosexuality as the only sin or the worst sin, or other things that the Bible doesn't say.

When I speak, I tell women this cautionary tale of Alex Hamilton and his wife. Because I know that mothers who keep their children from their fathers will always live to regret it. That's a fact—either their children will one day blame them or the women will come to the realization that they cheated their children. Either way, that's some place where a mother should never be.

I tell mothers that they need to let the father be as involved as he wants to be in his children's life. Women must find a way to learn to respect their father and his lifestyle. She doesn't have to agree with it, but she has to be respectful.

She has to be...all for the sake of the children.

CHAPTER 29

Gay Access

While I've had to deal with the haters over the course of these ten years, I've also met some very interesting people. For some reason, men open up to me. Maybe it's because of how I opened up with my book and on *Oprah*. Whatever the reason, several high profile men have talked to me about their sexuality and choice of lifestyle.

These men never had a problem being around me or letting me into their world. I attended party after party with men who were recognizable by most people. Gay athletes. Gay singers. Gay actors. Gay politicians. Gay executives. I've seen these men do all kinds of things. And though, I will never share a name nor an activity, I remember the first time I went to one of these high-level sex parties.

It was a party in NYC hosted by a popular entertainer who was known for his sex parties. His parties were always red-carpet affairs for powerful, public men who needed this privacy.

When I arrived and stepped into the huge condo on the 48th floor, I was immediately in awe of the breathtaking view of the city. But before I got too far into the apartment, I was told that I had to check my cell phone. There would be no picture taking nor video making at this event.

After that, I stepped inside and was blown away. Not only by the luxurious apartment and the spread of food that was on the buffet table, but I was shocked by the men who were there. I recognized just about every single one of them.

The wait staff and bartenders moved among us with trays of drinks and hors d'oeuvres—all great looking young men dressed only in jock straps.

The host greeted me, thanked me for coming, and then introduced me to the ten or so men who were there, though like I said, for me no introductions were necessary.

"This is the New York Times bestselling author JL King. You may have seen him on *Oprah*."

He took me around and introduced me to every man, telling them all that I was a good friend and could definitely be trusted. So he asked them all to welcome me to their inner circle. And every man greeted me like I was already one of them.

"Welcome," each of them said.

A couple of the men added that they were fans and had purchased my books for their wives or girlfriends. One of the men was a movie producer and he told me that my story would be great on the big screen.

I chatted with all of the men, and after a couple of drinks and some drugs that the host supplied, everybody was definitely loose. After we ate, the men began pairing up and walking off, disappearing throughout the condo.

I wasn't sure if I should approach anyone, but while I sat there trying to decide, everyone had gone off—except for one dude. But the great thing was, if there as anyone that I would've approached, he would've been the one.

He was a very attractive radio personality and we'd been eyeing each other all night. The sexual vibe between us built throughout the night, and I knew he had to feel it, too.

He came up to me and asked, "Do you want to go to one of the bedrooms and talk?"

"Yeah," I said.

I followed him through one of the long hallways since it seemed like he knew where he was going. Inside the bedroom, we sat down under the pretense of talking, but it wasn't very long before he got to the reason why we were back there.

"You know I don't just want to talk, right?" he said.

"I figured that."

"I've been a fan since I first saw you on TV and I've been following you ever since."

"Thanks."

"But it's more than that. From the first time I saw you on TV, I wanted you."

Not only was I flattered, but this was blowing my mind. I listened to this guy on the radio and he knew me?

He asked if he could perform oral sex on me and what was I supposed to say? As he got down on his knees, I couldn't believe that this man, who was one of the most prominent and powerful DJs in the country was enjoying me this way.

After we finished, we did talk, and he told me more about the group of men who were at this party.

"We get together often, our bond is tight. So if there is anything you ever need from one of us, you've got it."

"Thanks," I said.

The gathering lasted through the night. About 7am, breakfast was served and after that, the host escorted each man out, but he asked me to stay behind.

"So, what did you think, J?" he asked once we were alone.

"It was great. Thanks for inviting me."

He nodded. "I was glad to have you here. Your message is so needed. And, I wanted you to meet some men who understood why you wrote your book. They may not have told you, but some of them have used your book to help inform their love ones about men like them. That's why I wanted you to meet these men. Men who appreciated you because I know there are so many who have given you a hard time for speaking the truth."

"Thank you for saying that and for inviting me."

"You are always welcome here. And you can count on me for anything."

I appreciated being included with such a group of men. And I appreciated that they trusted me, knowing I would never reveal a single identity even though I've had sex with many of these men.

That doesn't mean, however, that I couldn't use some of my experiences with these men—and I have. I used the above experience in my novel, *Love on a Two Way Street*. After Wendy Williams read the book, the quote that she gave to my publisher and we put on the back cover was:

Is JL telling us fiction or non-fiction?

Well, now you know. That novel was written from personal experience. It was fiction written from fact.

I left that party feeling good, and over the years, I've called on some of the men that I met there that night. So, when I am asked how do I get all of this media attention all the time... now, you know.

CHAPTER 30

The Things Men Need to Know

Being a gay man...

I know that it is hard enough being a man in this world, and to be a gay man quadruples the challenges. So much so that many men prefer not to admit nor accept their sexuality. Many men choose to stay on the DL because they know they will never be accepted by their friends and family. And if he's black, he may never be accepted by his community.

If I could shout one message from the rooftops, it would be this—you cannot change who you are, and no one can change you. So you must find a way to accept yourself. This is something that I've always believed and it became painfully obvious with the story of a young man who'd been in my life for a while.

I'd met Tony when he was just fifteen years old and when he was twenty, he told me that he thought he was bisexual.

"I'm attracted to both men and women. What should I do?" he asked me.

"Why should you have to do anything?" I asked.

"I have to do something because my parents will never accept it. My mom is always talking about when I get married, and when I start having children."

"Well, you said you were bisexual...."

"Yeah, but I can't be with men at all. My dad hates people who are gay. You should hear how he talks about homosexuals."

I remember the way Tony shuddered as he told me that and then he went on to say that he was going to have to do what he could to please his parents.

"They're all that matter."

I tried to convince him that *he* mattered, but he was convinced that his parent's feelings were more important than his own.

A few years later, Tony started seriously dating a women he'd met at school, and when he told me about it, I asked him was he happy?

"No! I mean, she's nice and everything; she's the perfect girl for my parents. She's the kind of girl that my mom and dad would want me to marry."

"But your parents aren't dating her, your parents aren't going to marry her."

"I know," he said shaking his head. "And I've read enough of your books and heard you speak enough to know this isn't right, but what else can I do? I don't have any choice. Because of my parents."

I couldn't get him to stop focusing on his parents. "You do have choices. You can do the right thing."

"And the right thing will hurt my parents."

I told him that I understood his feelings and his pain. "But I know you, Tony. I know you don't want to destroy her life."

"I don't want to do that, but...."

"One day, you're going to cheat on her...with a man. Trust me, I know. No matter how hard you fight it, your feelings will win out. The best thing to do is to tell her the truth and tell your parents, too."

All Tony did was shake his head. "You don't know what it's like, JL. You don't know what it's like to have everyone expecting something of you."

"Well then, don't get married. Stay single. But don't bring this innocent girl into this."

He listened to me that night, but his parents' will for his life was stronger than my words. And about a year later, I heard that Tony was engaged and six months later, married.

I prayed for him, knowing that a bitter end was coming. I just didn't know how bitter it was going to be.

Just a few months after his wedding, Tony called me, crying hysterically.

"I cheated on her, JL. I did it with this guy that I work out with at the gym."

I did my best to calm him down and not say 'I told you so.' All I told him over and over was, "I understand. I understand."

"But if she finds out, she won't understand. And neither will my mother or father. Oh, God! My father! My father is going to hate me!"

"He's not."

"Yes, he is, you just don't know."

I talked to Tony for another hour, but he was still crying when he hung up. Two days later, I received another call from a mutual friend. Tony had gone home that night and shot himself in the head. The pressure of what he'd done—getting married to a woman, then cheating with a man—was more than he could stand.

There is so much blame to go around for Tony. From his parents to society—we don't give people in this country room to be who they are. Blessedly, things are changing, but still there are people who need to really look at their feelings about gay men and women. They need to ask themselves how can they hate so much when they've never walked in a gay person's shoes?

It is our reaction to homosexuals that has young men and women committing suicide. It is our reaction to homosexuals that has men doing whatever they can to stay in the closet and protecting their images by having sex with women. If we continue to ostracize these men and women, then we can't say a word about the state of black women being the fastest growing group of new HIV cases.

This is something that we have to think about because whether we like it or not, we are all in this together. We are all affected by how gay men choose to live their lives. And the next man who wants to kill himself, just might be someone that you know...or love.

Being a Gay Father....

In the beginning while I always wanted to be with my children, there were times when I put my life in front of theirs. There were times when a date, or a party or my current man distracted me from doing what was right for Ebony and Brandon.

When I look back on those days, I am so sorry. I hate who I was, I hate that I didn't keep my role as a father first over everything else. The men I was with during those times are no longer in my life, but my children are. And they're there all... the...time. That's a blessing to me.

Please do not do what I did. I allowed my sexuality and my lifestyle to stop me from being the best father that I could be. I was discovering myself then; I didn't even really know who I was, so I wasn't sure that I had anything to offer my son and daughter. But boy, was I wrong. My children could have helped me become more centered, quicker. There is nothing like what a child can bring into your life, and no love can compare to the love a child can give. And think about all that you have to offer your sons and your daughters. Don't leave them behind.

It hasn't been easy, but I've remained in my children's lives and I think this was particularly important for my son. Along with his mother, I've raised my son to be a respectful, responsible young man. Of course, he heard the messages from his mother, but he heard my voice as well.

Because of the lessons I've learned, I founded The National Black Gay Fathers Association, an organization for gay fathers who want to be in the lives of their children. My organization provides not only information, but support for gay fathers who may have to fight their exes to see their children. We give advice and help to any man who is having his sexual orientation used against him.

Founding this organization is just my way of using my experience to give back to others. But it's also because of the stories I'd heard that I knew this association was needed.

A few years ago, I met a twenty-two-year-old man who was the father of three-year-old twin girls. But not too long after the girls were born, he came out as a gay man.

Of course, this infuriated his ex and her family and they did everything they could to try to keep him out of his daughters' lives. They threatened to expose him to his friends and family. That didn't work because he'd come out already and his family supported him.

Next, his ex tried to get a court order to keep him away from his girls, but that didn't work. They tried everything, from starting rumors to making threats—things that really hurt this man to his core. No matter what they did, though, he stood tall, fought hard, and kept his rights to be his daughters' father.

"I fought with everything I had in me," he told me. "Because my girls mean everything and I'm going to be there for them no matter what. I want to be at every PTA meeting, every dance recital. I want to be there when they start dating, and I'm going to walk them down the aisle when they get married."

"Good for you!" I said, so proud of this young, gay brother who was determined to take care of business.

"But the only thing...I wish that I'd had a role model, or some other support as I was going through all of this. Sure, my parents were there, but they're not gay. I needed a gay role model. Someone who was already doing it and who could have helped me go through."

That was the story that got my gears going. I imagined that there were thousands of young fathers just like him who had not fought as hard as he did. I was sure there were young brothers who gave in under the threat of blackmail or being exposed to people at work, or at church. So, they just gave up their parental rights. It was this kind of man that I wanted to help.

I pray for the day when a person is not judged on their sexuality. But until that time, I'm going to use my life as an open book to help other fathers. I'm going to keep fighting so that our children can grow up knowing the love of both of their parents.

Stop the madness....

I understand why men lie, I understand why men choose to live their lives on the down-low, but here's what I also know. These men who are lying have sisters, aunts, cousins, and maybe even their mother—women who are out there meeting men. How would any of these men feel if the women they loved were being lied to?

Well, the woman that you're lying to is someone's sister, aunt, cousin, mother.

I don't care if you're sixteen or one-hundred-and-six; if you're lying about your sexuality...stop the madness! Because the person that you're cheating on probably looks a lot like a woman that you love. Hopefully, this is something that men will start to really think about so that we can turn this whole thing about unsuspecting women being infected around.

CHAPTER 31

The Things that Women Need to Know

Stop being desperate...

*I*f I had a dollar for every time a woman asked me how could she tell whether or not her man was gay, I could retire right now and move to Dubai. But besides the answer to that question, there are so many other things that I want to share with women. Things that I've learned as a gay man. Things I've learned as women, who knew I was gay, still offer themselves to me.

My first piece of advice: Stop being desperate. Stop giving away your love, your body, your emotions, and your spirit to men who mean you no good.

This is what I tell my daughter. Ebony is almost forty, and wonderfully fabulous. She's educated, very attractive, has a great home, is enjoying life...and is single. We often talk about her fear of never being married, never having children. And she's afraid that she won't be happy. Of course, every father wants nothing but happiness for his daughter.

But I tell her what I just told you—don't be desperate!

Because it is the desperate woman who is most vulnerable to the shady guy, to the down low guy. Of course this is not every case and it wasn't the case with my ex-wife. With Brenda, she and I were high school sweethearts and after that, I became a seasoned, skilled liar.

But in today's times, men who are trying to keep their sexuality a secret prey on desperate women and here's why. These men know that a woman who is desperate to have a man, will not ask as many questions and will look the other way if she has to. There are even some desperate women who will stay in an unfulfilled or even abusive relationship, just so she can say, "I have a man."

These men will prey on women like that and you won't even see them coming. Why not? Because they don't "act gay." They're not out doing the things that straight people think gay men do. These men are not in gay clubs and are not hanging out at gay events. They're wherever you are—at the gym, at the mall, at church!

And these men don't "look gay." These players are good looking, smooth brothers who will tell you that they adore their mothers and that they love being fathers. The dudes will tell you that they are looking for the love of their lives, when all they're really searching for is you—if you're a desperate woman. If you are not aware, these men appear to be the perfect catch.

Sisters, let me tell you this right now—you don't *need* a man. You don't need a man to be complete or happy. Learn to love yourself first, and then, you will attract love...the right kind of love.

Now, let's say that you have found what you think is the right kind of love. Here's the thing—in today's times, you have to put on your investigative reporter hat. You have to ask questions and you must get answers.

First of all, never, ever have sex with any man without seeing his *latest* HIV test results. Seriously, do not have any kind of sex, not oral, not vaginal, not anal. And don't be afraid to ask because that fear could lead you to a death sentence.

Now once you've seen his clean bill of health, it's time for the talk. It may be hard to do, but you have to talk to your potential sex partner about his sexual past. And I mean, you really must have a good heart-to-heart talk with the brother.

I've mentioned this to women in the seminars I've done and many women have written me, inquiring, "What should I ask a man?"

Well ask him everything you can think of, and then ask these ten questions that I've told my daughter to ask any man who thinks he's worthy of her:

1. Have you ever wanted to have sex with a man?
2. Have you ever had sex with a man?
3. Do you watch gay porn?

4. How would you feel if I answered your cell phone or read your text messages?
5. What would you think about me having the password to your email and you having the password to mine?
6. What turns you on in bed?
7. What turns you off in bed?
8. What are your greatest fears?
9. Can we talk about everything?
10. Do you believe in the power of prayer?

Now, I'm not saying that the answer to whether or not a man is on the down low or secretly gay will be determined by his answers to these questions. But I am saying that this will get the conversation going—a conversation that too many women are afraid to have.

Don't be desperate! Get the answers you need to stay alive.

There is no need to label every man as gay....

Boy, is this a hot button topic and very touchy for some women. I cannot tell you the number of debates I've been in with women who have told me that if a man is sleeping with a man, he's gay—period! Even if he says he likes women.

And my response to that is always—wrong!

There really are men (and women) who are bisexual, who can truly enjoy sex with a man or a woman equally. And if this is a touchy subject for straight woman, it's just as touchy for a bisexual man because he doesn't want to be labeled as gay.

That was my situation at first. From the bottom of my heart I didn't think I was gay because I equally enjoyed men and women. But over the years I realized that I had to make a choice because my behavior was hurting women and I couldn't continue that way. I didn't want to be a liar and live a life of lies.

But that was my choice and I don't judge any man who doesn't feel he wants to nor has to do the same thing that I did. Especially since there are men who cannot even have sex with another man without watching porn featuring women. Many of these men will not kiss another man, and will even keep touching to a minimum. Their behavior is very different than mine, so why do they have to be labeled as gay, straight, or anything?

Like I said, it's a hot topic, especially with women. But I always ask if a woman is having sex with women and men, does that make her a lesbian? I can never quite get a "straight" answer to that question.

I get the need for people to label other people. That's what makes us comfortable. But the truth is, like most things in life, this is not black or white—like life, this is gray. And on a sexual scale of one to ten, most of us are not ones (completely straight) nor tens (completely gay). We all fall along that spectrum.

The best thing all of us can do is stop putting labels on people. Let's just all be honest with who we are, and then men and women can make the grown up, personal decisions about who they want to be with and who they do not.

You Better Check Yourself, Before You Wreck Yourself

I'm going to say this as simply as I can...use condoms!

In this day and time, I'm amazed at the number of grown women who will allow a man to go into them without a condom. But from what my friends tell me, and from my own experience, that's most women. And here's the thing...so many men, men who are on the down low or men who are out as bisexual, do not practice safe sex.

That sounds crazy, right? Well, that's one of the reasons why I became a successful HIV speaker. I went around to organizations and told people this. I tried to break through to the experts, letting them know that their message wasn't reaching men like me. When I was first out there, being wild, I didn't know my HIV status and I didn't care. And my friends were the same way.

Here's why—HIV had nothing to do with us. We weren't gay, remember? And HIV/AIDS is a gay disease.

There are probably people reading this and laughing out loud right now, but I'm telling you there are still so many men who not only think this, but they believe it...right down to their soul. And while you're laughing, these men are having sex with someone you know.

Women, it's up to you. Unless you're married, you should never have sex without a condom. (And there are many married women who should do the same, but that's a different book!) It's your responsibility: bring the condoms, check the condoms, use the condoms. Or else, there is a high, high chance that you will one day regret it.

Don't play Russian roulette with your life.

You cannot change a gay man...and why would you want to anyway....

Do you know how many times women ask me to go out with them? Or what's even more shocking—I've even had a few marriage proposals. Seriously. From women. Who know I'm gay!

It started right after my *Oprah* appearance. I would show up to events and women would send me notes to meet them after the event for dinner...and much more. When I first moved to Atlanta, I had as much sex with women as I did with men.

Sisters told me all kinds of things.

"All you have to do is taste this pussy...."

"Let me put it on you and I guarantee that you will never go back...."

"You just haven't found the right woman yet...."

And every time all I could say was, "Huh? Do you know who I am?"

And now, social media has made it worse. From Facebook to Twitter, I get all kinds of invitations. Recently a sister inboxed me on Facebook and told me that she knew for a fact that I wanted her and she wanted me. So we needed to stop playing, get together, and have sex.

Huh? Do you know who I am?

At first, I used to wonder what in the world was going on? But after a while, I got it. Yes, women were sure that they could change me, but there were also many things that they found attractive about me. First of all, I'd been open and up front about my sexuality—well, at least I was once I wrote that book. And I believe that:

1. These women found my honesty a turn-on.
2. They knew what they were getting and were willing to deal with it.
3. It was their choice, their decision and many may have found that challenge sexy.
4. They were turned on by trying to turn me on.
5. They figure that I'm rich and they'll take the money and deal with everything else later.
6. They respected me for being real.
7. They were risk takers and loved the challenge.
8. They loved my swagger and good looks. (Okay, that may sound a bit self-serving, but I believe that's true.)

But if you don't believe me, there is one incident that happened to me that really brought my theory to light.

On one of my tour stops in Detroit, there was a woman who hung around, staring at me as I signed books and chatted with other women. I had already signed her book and we'd talked for a moment, but even as I moved on to others in the line, she hung around.

It wasn't hard to notice her because she stood out. She was very attractive, in her mid-40s, and was dressed in an expensive designer knit suit. It must have been the "I still like women" spirit in my eyes that made her stay behind.

At the end of the event, the coordinator called her over and reintroduced me, "JL, this is Angela; she's going to take you to your hotel."

That was cool with me because out of everyone there, she was someone that I didn't mind talking to. We chatted easily in the car ride and as she pulled up to the hotel, she asked, "Do you have any plans tonight?"

I shook my head. "Nope. Just dinner. Room service. My flight leaves at six in the morning, so I'm going to get some rest."

"Oh, that's too bad. I really wanted to take you out to dinner...would you like to go?"

I thought about it for a moment. I wasn't tired, and there were lots of things that were worse than spending time with a good-looking, smart sister.

"Okay, give me about an hour."

I went up to my room, did my thing, and came back to the lobby an hour later. And Angela was right there. She'd apparently gone home to change and boy did she look sexy in her red pants suit that accentuated her 5'8" 130 pound frame. And her hair, her locs were tied high on her head.

All I could think of was…sexy. This woman was…stunning!

"Hey, you," she said as she came over and hugged me. "You look good."

"I always look good," I kidded. "You never know…I might meet a fine brother who'll want to come back to the hotel with me tonight."

I laughed. She didn't.

She said, "Well, my favorite seafood restaurant is right down the street and we can walk; is that okay with you?"

"Sure."

On the walk over, we went back into our chatting mode, but this time her questions were specific and interesting.

"How did you become gay?"

"Do you think you'll always be gay?"

"Don't you want to be married again?"

I answered every one of her questions as honestly as I could. I figured that she was trying to get as much information out of me as she could. Maybe she had a boyfriend and she was trying to determine if he were gay or straight.

All through the candle-lit dinner (okay, yes, I missed that) we chatted about my life, especially my life on the down low until finally, she said, "JL, I would love to spend the night with you."

Huh? Do you know who I am?

Of course, that's not what I said out loud, but I'm sure that was the look on my face. I had just told this woman that I loved men and that I would never marry a woman again, that I was sure that my future was with a man.

I was speechless.

So, since I didn't say anything, she did. "I find you very sexy and I know having sex with you would be amazing."

Finally, I found my voice. "Angela, I'm really touched, but we both know that I'm into men."

"I know that's what you say, but I feel our connection and I could be that woman that changes you."

No! I screamed inside.

She said, "And if I couldn't change you, I would just let you do your thing on the side."

"Let me do my thing?"

"Yeah, I know that you're bisexual, and I have no problem with that if you want to continue. We'd just have to establish some rules."

"Wow!"

"Look, I'm just being open and honest. Do you know how many men I've been with who have lied to me and cheated on me with women?" She shrugged. "At least with you, I know what I'm getting. I know who you are and you're not hiding. So to me, you'd be a great man to be with now...and maybe even become a great husband."

"Angela, I don't know what to say."

"Think about it...how many women would make this offer to you? Would let you still have sex with men, and still love you? The only thing is that I don't want to know who you're sexing; I wouldn't want you to bring that home. But besides that, I would be fine with everything."

At first, I wondered if this was some kind of joke, but the way she looked into my eyes, with innocent, honest eyes, I knew she was serious.

After a long moment of silence, I said, "I can't do that to you."

"You wouldn't be doing anything to me that I didn't agree to."

"But suppose I met a man that I really wanted to be with."

"I told you, I'm fine with that. You would just be with both of us." She covered my hand with hers. "I'm different, JL. Just let me show you."

"It wouldn't work."

"Well, that's because you think you'll find a man. But honestly, I don't think that's going to be a problem. Once you've had sex with me, you won't want anyone else."

I didn't want to hurt her feelings, but I wanted to ask her about all of those men that she'd had sex with in the past who had sex with other women. *They* wanted someone else.

She said, "I can change you. Just give me a chance. I can change your being gay."

Those words turned me right off. Not that I was ever going to do anything with her anyway, but she had just told me that she was going to change me when I was happy with who I was. I didn't ask to be, and didn't want to be changed. Now she was trying to play God. Because if I needed to be changed, God was the only one who could change me.

"Who said I wanted to be changed?" I asked her. "I'm happy being gay. I was born this way; God created me."

"But...."

I held up my hand, stopping her. "I think you're a great lady, and we can be friends, but that's it."

I guess she finally got my point because tears welled up in her eyes, and I felt sorry. I hadn't been trying to hurt her, but when she started talking that 'I can change you' stuff, I was over it.

She nodded like she finally understood and I reached over and kissed her hand. "You're beautiful and I hope we'll be friends for a long, long time."

The walk back to the hotel was a silent one and I could feel Angela's hurt. I said, "Do you want to spend the night with me?"

She looked up at me with hopeful eyes.

"Did you ever see *Waiting to Exhale*?"

She nodded, but frowned.

"Remember Wesley Snipes and Angela Bassett. Sleep only."

For the first time in a while, she smiled. "Okay."

And that is exactly what happened. She came to my room, we laid on the bed together and it felt wonderful just holding her as we both fell into a deep sleep.

That night, Angela got the message and I hope you will, too. You cannot change a man. Not any man. And you especially cannot change a gay man's sexuality.

Ladies, you can't compete with another man....

There is one question that women ask me that comes with all kinds of attitude...I mean, the neck-rolling and the duck-lips. With all kinds of disgust in their tone, women ask me, "What can a man do for my man that I can't?"

Here's the thing—you will never be able to compete with a man for your man. No way, so don't even try. Just give it up. And here's why:

Men who enjoy sex with men:

1. Love the feel of the hardness of a man. (You can't give him that.)
2. Love the smell and scent of a man. (You can't give him that.)

3. Love the power of sex between men. (You can't give him that.)

4. Feel having sex (particularly with an older man) can somehow fill the void of their missing father. (I know, that's not good—but you can't give him that.)

5. Love being submissive to another man. (You can't give him that.)

6. Love having oral sex from a man because his jaws are so much stronger than a woman's. (You can't give him that.).

7. Love the masculinity of men and that turns them on. It is a male bonding thing. (You can't give him that.)

8. Feel safe when they are with another man sexually. (You can't give him that.)

9. Love the fact they can have sex with another man because it's so illicit. (You can't give him that.)

10. Love that men are not as emotional and won't get attached. (Okay, you may be able to give him that, but after the other nine points....)

And, I can back up these facts with this story:

I have a friend who plays for the NBA. He is one of those larger-than-life sex symbols with a swagger that woman love. He has a beautiful girlfriend, two children with her...yet he is a man who loves to be submissive to other men. Maybe this is because he always has to be the one in charge. With his overly masculine image, he is a leader, both on and off the court. But in the bedroom, he enjoys reversing that role.

Maybe he can't do that with his woman, so he does it with his man. When he's away from his girlfriend, he plays "wifey" to his boyfriend. He likes being told what to do, he likes calling his man, "Daddy." I've been to their home and when he's around his boyfriend, he is nothing like his public persona. He told me that he loves giving up the power that he always has to exert at home and on the court. But with his man, he can just chill. And he told me that of course, he loves the sex. He loves the masculine connection.

So when he goes back home, he's relaxed, refreshed and a better man for his girlfriend and children—at least that's what he truly believes.

I understand everything that he told me because I walked in his shoes. My challenge with this is that he is not giving his girlfriend a chance to decide if she wants to share her man with a man. But this is how he's chosen to live and trust me, he is not the only one in the NBA...or the NFL...or in MLB... and it goes on and on and on.

The reason I have such a difficult time getting through to a man like him is that he doesn't think he's cheating on his girlfriend. But I will always try to convince these men to be truthful. Because once a woman finds out, she's traumatized for a long, long time.

When a beautiful young woman at Howard University came up to me after a lecture and told me that she'd caught her boyfriend in bed with his best friend, she was so hurt that she promised she would never have sex again.

"And then, I found out that this had been going on all along. I don't understand it. I thought it was women who I had to compete with. He was such a ladies man and always talked about how he hated gay men. He told so many lies, I don't think I'll ever be able to trust a man again!"

"Don't say that. You can't judge every man by his actions," I told her.

"But how will I know? There are probably not that many straight men left."

I told her that I didn't think that was true, but that she should just use this as a lesson. "Find out all you can about potential boyfriends. Ask questions, be nosey, and take your time. Don't just fall in love and give yourself so quickly."

My greatest fear was that this beautiful, twenty-two-year-old sister was going to give up on finding love. That broke my heart.

I don't want women to give up on men. Especially black men. We need more married couples raising children in a two-parent household. I want my nieces and cousins and girlfriends to be married to a man who will love only them, but just as important will not lie to them. For the rest of my life, I will be an advocate for honest, open relationships—something that I always didn't do, but I thank God that I found my way.

CHAPTER 32

The Journey to this Place in my Life...

*T*here were many good things that happened for me in Atlanta, but even though I tried to stay connected to God, between the money and the life, I lost my way. I really did. Over the years, it became worse and worse. I was spending money like water, I was lending thousands to people who said they would pay me back, but would then disappear, I was being used by folks that I thought were my friends. But the hardest part of all, was that I was still being demonized—by the media, Internet bloggers, and my enemies—as the lying, cheating down-low brother. There were so many negative things being written and said about me, I didn't even recognize the person they said I was.

In the beginning, I was able to ignore most of the talk and the people who I found out were just using me. But it began to weigh on me, and became so heavy, that I fell into a depression. There came a time when all I would do was wake up in the morning, go to Starbucks, take my dog to the park, call the guy I was sexing, have sex with him all day, then spend all night drinking and doing drugs. That became my life—I did little else.

And the more I lived like that—Starbucks, sex all day, drugs all night—the more depressed I became. It was a vicious cycle that left me in a complete mess.

I tried to fight my way out of my hopelessness, but I couldn't do it. No matter what, I couldn't find a way. All I thought about was just how sad my life had become. And thoughts like that sent me spiraling further downward.

I began to think that the only solution, the only way out was to end it all. Like the other dark times in my life, suicide became my option and thoughts of how I could take my life consumed me.

I was in a really bad place one day when my daughter Ebony called and even though I didn't want to burden her, there was no one else in the world that I could talk to.

I told her of my troubles, I told her how depressed I was, I told her...that I'd contemplated suicide.

"Daddy, no!"

"I know, baby girl," I cried. "I know it's wrong, but I just don't know what else to do. I'm just so unhappy."

"Well, maybe God's trying to get your attention. Maybe you've become too complacent and God wants you to leave Atlanta to do something else."

I listened to my daughter, listened to her wisdom, and when we finally hung up, I talked to God for the first time in a long time. I got down on my knees and asked Him, "God, what is it that you want me to do?"

And just like God had done before when He told me to tell my story. He came to me, this time in a dream. But even though my eyes were closed and I knew I was asleep, His words and His message were clear.

I want you to sell everything...give up everything. Everything. Trust me. Sell everything.

When I woke up the next morning, there were no thoughts of suicide in my mind. All I could hear was the voice of God and what He wanted me to do.

I called my daughter and told her that after I spoke with her, I prayed. And then, I told her about my dream.

"I agree," she said. "Sell or give away everything. Don't try to pack a microwave, don't try to take a couch. Just do what God told you to do!"

I hung up from my daughter and went to work. I called friends, acquaintances, colleagues, the Salvation Army, Good Will—and told them what I was doing, and asked them what did they want.

I followed God's directive. I sold some things, but I gave just about everything I owned away. I had an extensive library of over five thousand books that I divided between a church and a few of my friends. I had a half-million dollar art collection that I gave away to friends.

I made it my mission to do what God told me to do; I was determined to let go. Within two weeks, I had given away just about all that I had.

Ebony kept calling me, giving me her support. I had yet to decide where I was going or what I was going to do, but then my daughter encouraged me.

"Daddy, you should go to New York."

I had always wanted to live in New York, but living in that city was expensive. I had never wanted to move there without a place to live and a job or business opportunity waiting for me.

But when my daughter said that to me, I considered it. My son and his wife-to-be, lived there as well as one of my exes who I was still friends with. I would be taking a huge step of faith by leaving Atlanta, the place that I'd called home for more than ten years. But with what I'd just experienced the last two weeks, I was already operating on faith. So what could a little move to New York City do to me?

All that I had left in Atlanta were things that I called family valuables—photos and other mementos that meant so much to me. I put all of that in storage, leaving me with just three suitcases of personal belongings, but I was ready to go.

Within a month of having that dream, it was goodbye Atlanta and hello, New York.

Yes, my son was in New York, but I didn't want to live with him. So I called up my ex and just like I expected, he invited me to stay with him for a while. I was set!

It was nighttime, when I flew into New York with my three suitcases, excited once again about my life and the possibilities. I'd never been to my ex's place before and was surprised when the cab slowed down in the Crown Heights section of Brooklyn. I didn't have to be a native New Yorker to figure out that this wasn't one of the best neighborhoods, but I was going to stay positive.

My ex was glad to see me. He invited me into his rather small, one-bedroom apartment, but still, I stayed positive. My plan wasn't to be there for too long. This was just a pit-stop until I could get situated and I'd start making money for myself.

My friend told me that I could use his bed since he was going to have a few friends over. I didn't think any of that until I got up in the middle of the night to use the restroom. When I opened the bedroom door and walked into the hallway, I stopped dead in my tracks.

From where I stood, I could see straight into the living room. There were five naked people there—four women and one guy—and from what I could tell, they were cooking crack! Across the room from them, was my friend—naked and smoking a crack pipe!

I went into shock!

Rushing back into the bedroom, I locked the door, then texted him. I told him that I was going to call the police if he didn't get those people out of the apartment. I didn't care that it wasn't my place, but I wasn't about to be sitting up in some kind of drug house.

About twenty minutes later, I heard the front door open, close, and then quick steps coming toward the bedroom.

My friend knocked on the door and called out my name at the same time. When I opened the door, he apologized. "They just asked me if they could use my place, but I promise you, that won't happen again."

Well, he didn't have anyone back at his place cooking crack anymore, but what I didn't realize until then was that my friend's life was really messed up. He was a crackhead who lived to have sex with men day and night to pay for his habit.

Every night, there was a steady stream of men coming to his apartment. One at a time, two at a time—it didn't matter, my ex had sex with all of them. One night, there had to be six men who fucked him. All while he smoked crack.

There were days when it went on and on. And I was so afraid. Not only of the people who were in and out of the apartment, but I was even afraid to leave my things there.

The thing that was so f'up about what my friend was doing, was that he was an HIV positive man who had unprotected sex every night. I saw it. But not only that, the next morning, he'd get up, go to work as an administrative assistant at the largest HIV prevention agency in Manhattan!

Seriously! During the day, this man talked to men about safe sex and HIV prevention, but at night, he was a spreader of the virus. And what was worse, he used his position to get men. Just like I used to do—he used his job to meet men. Men who came to him as clients, looking for education and condoms.

I had to get out of there and away from him. I had no choice; I had to call my son who was so glad to come for me.

"You can stay with me for as long as you need to, Dad," he said.

I was grateful for that. I just wanted to stay with him long enough to learn the city and get my feet wet.

Once I was with Brandon, I relaxed and got down to the business of loving New York. I loved everything about the city: the energy, the potpourri of cultures, the variety of foods and even, dare I say it—the subways. I loved riding the subway, watching people, listening to the different accents and seeing the different personalities. To me, the people who made up the city were beautiful.

And, don't even get me started on the shopping.

I began to learn the different parts of New York and Harlem became one of my favorite hangouts. I would head up to one of the bars and just people watch. And it gave me the opportunity to meet people and make friends. I started being invited to social events: art openings, plays...or just plain parties. I was finally coming alive once again.

But the best part of being in New York was being with my son, Brandon. I loved spending time with him in his beautiful apartment in Fort Green. For the first time, I felt like a full-time father. We had nothing but time to spend together and bond the way I always believed a father and son should. His girlfriend was pregnant at the time, and we talked about him becoming a father and the joy that this new King would bring to our family.

But we also talked business. If there is one thing that he got from me, it's his desire to be an entrepreneur. He had the same hustling spirit that I had and I encouraged him in his business.

It didn't take long for me to begin to see why God had moved me to New York. I thanked Him every day for taking me away from Atlanta and putting me in a place that gave me life and showed me that life is about living and not just existing.

Moving to New York saved me, and living there is a dream come true. This hasn't been an easy transition—New Yorkers don't care about JL King. Author who? New York Times Bestseller what? I have to put in the time, pay my dues, and earn my way just like every other New Yorker.

And so besides working hard, I have to depend on my faith to survive. I am truly focusing on what I've told others—

having faith over fear. I understand that you have to do more than just say it, you have to live it. Faith is an action word, it's a verb. My faith is movement.

And now because I've accepted and understand this, life is good. I am happy. I feel like my life is complete. I have lived my life's purpose and I know that I'm blessed to be able to say that because there are many who can't. I'm building a legacy that I will be able to leave not only for my children and grandchildren, but for many others who learned lessons or were saved by one of my books or lectures. It has been a tough road, but not only am I glad that God told me to tell my story, I am glad that I was obedient.

I can look back and see God at work in my life. The way he took me through valleys when He needed to get my attention, and then the way He picked me up when I didn't think there was any way to come up from being so low. Through it all He was there. Even when I was angry, mad, sad, even when I was doubting His existence, He never left my side.

My prayer from today until the day I die is that I will continue to live with this faith, that I will continue to trust God. I pray that I will always be thankful and grateful to Him for forgiving me for my sins, especially the lying and deception that was so much a part of me.

And now, I can celebrate. Not because I am finished. I know there is still much work to do. But, I can celebrate because the truth has set me free. I can celebrate because God is always with me. I can celebrate because I survived.

Truly, my life has come full circle.

AFTERWORD

When I started this book, I told close friends and family that I was done. Done writing books, done with trying to be a publisher, and done with trying to help other writers become authors. All of it was too hard and required too much time. Because of my past and my success, authors expected me to make them an instant best seller or get them on *Oprah* or *Wendy*.

Well in today's market, that's not going to happen, so I decided that I would just sit back and enjoy the fruits of *Full Circle's* success. I had made plans, too: I was going to travel to South Africa and spend a month there in December. Then, I was going to come back and teach a creative writing class. And maybe I would even get the opportunity to work with Brown Girls Publishing/Brown Girls Books beyond *Full Circle* because I believe in their mission and I know they will be successful.

But you know what? I read long time ago that when man plans, God laughs. And I can tell you now, that is so true. The moment I had the rest of my career-life plan in place, I met this sister. Now let me tell you this first—for years, people have told me that I needed to write about women who are on the down low because if you didn't know, there are women who live on the down low, too. I've always said that that wasn't my story—a DL woman would have to write that.

Well now, as my life has come full circle, she shows up. I met a woman who's been living on the DL for years. Just like me she hid her life, told lies to cover up her deception, lived in denial, and now she's ready to tell it all.

Her book, titled *Not Just For Men—My Life as a Down Low Sister*, will be co-written by me. And I'm so excited about this because finally the world will be able to read the other story. People need to know that there are women leading double lives, too.

My hope is that *Not Just For Men* will help to free thousands, many of them whom I've met as I was taking my own full circle journey toward personal acceptance.

Once that project is complete, I'll be able to say that my destiny has been fulfilled. I will have completely obeyed God when He told me to tell my story. And in the legacy that God has guided me to fulfill, I hope that many will learn to live their lives in truth.

All I can say, all I will ever say, all I will continuously say is, "Thank you, Father for using me and truly making my circle complete."

CPSIA information can be obtained at www.ICGtesting.com
Printed in the USA
LVOW11s2119181214

419525LV00001B/39/P